WELCOME TO THE REAL WORLD

TIM FLOYD

BROADMAN PRESS
Nashville, Tennessee

Unless otherwise indicated, all Scriptures
are from the King James Version of the Bible.

All Scriptures marked NIV are from the HOLY BIBLE *New International Version,* copyright © 1978, New York Bible Society. Used by permission.

All Scriptures marked NASB are from the *New American Standard Bible.* Copyright © The Lockman Foundation, 1960, 1962, 1963, 1968, 1971, 1972, 1973, 1975, 1977. Used by permission.

Dewey Decimal Classification: 248.4
  Subject Heading: CHRISTIAN LIFE
Library of Congress Catalog Number: 84-5876
  Printed in the United States of America

Library of Congress Cataloging in Publication Data

Floyd, Tim, 1948-
  Welcome to the real world.

  1. Christian life—1960-   2. Christianity—
20th century.   I. Title.
BV4501.2.F575   1984   248   84-5876
ISBN 0-8054-5001-7

Dedication
To my wife and partner,
Jonnel

Foreword

In *Welcome to the Real World,* Tim Floyd makes a significant contribution in both diagnosis and prescription for the present malaise of the Church. His diagnosis of the underlying illness of the Church is "false perception." He correctly perceives that most people are responding not to reality but to illusion. This false perception of what is the ultimate reality and ultimate truth of the universe leads to catastrophic problems in the lives of both individuals and the Church collectively.

Since the natural man is blind and even the vision of Christians is obscured by the miasma of worldliness, what is needed, he writes, is a vision corrected by faith. Only then will we be able to walk the Christian pilgrimage; overcome the king of terror, death; and face the sufferings of this world. These and numerous other advantages flow from a vision corrected by faith.

For many people this book will be like putting on corrective glasses after seeing the world as a blur far too long. Like a skilled ophthalmologist, he has done his work well. If it is true that "in the valley of the blind, the one-eyed man is king," then those who are given clarity of vision in a world of the staggering blind will have entered into their kingly rights as the sons of Him who is light itself.

D. James Kennedy, Ph.D.
President, Evangelism Explosion International

Contents

1. Sleepwalk

From a child's viewpoint, the practice of sleepwalking can be filled with many perils. Chief among those is the potential for sudden, incomprehensible death by surprise. "Never wake a person who is walking in his sleep," so the saying goes, "or he'll have a heart attack and die!"

Of course, with the passing of childhood often comes the realization that somnambulism, however inexplicable, is for the most part a harmless phenomenon.

The most basic danger of sleepwalking stems from the individual's false frame of reference. In one's dream he sees and, consequently, responds to one particular set of stimuli, circumstances, and situations. But all the time, the unwary sleepwalker is moving among a completely different set of circumstances and properties—a *real* set. Difficulty arises when the dream suggests an open door where the real world offers a plate glass window. *Crash!*

As a yawning physician puts the final stitches in a throbbing face, even the groggy patient can plumb the depths of his dilemma. Through sleepwalking he has responded to an illusion, only to be injured by reality.

Then, is it any wonder that the concept of reality is often modified by such terms as *harsh, stark, bare,* and

11

painful? Doctors report that many emotionally disturbed individuals are actually behaving logically. They are responding to reality as they see it. Unfortunately, though, the majority of the world defines that reality differently.

In a cynical age when many have eagerly responded to the question, "What's wrong with the church?" consider yet one further diagnosis.

It has been said that the problem is due to a lack of repentance. Others have examined Christendom and noted a real drought in evangelism. Still others have discovered a callousness, an *unlovingness,* typified by a decline in social ministries. Not enough training! Insufficient prayer! Inadequate preaching!

Interestingly enough, all of these charges may be generally true, but ironically, they are all symptoms.

The doctor is correct when he stands at the bedside of a dying woman and says, "She has a fever." Correct he is, but helpful he isn't. Instead, the physician who would heal is the one who observes the fever, as well as all the other symptoms, and accurately diagnoses the illness. Only then can treatment be prescribed.

What then is the disease that has wrought such havoc in the body of Christ today? What malady could have rendered Christendom so unevangelistic, uncaring, and delirious, so generally anemic?

The conclusions that follow may sound too modernistic. They may not ring with the same authenticity as demands for revival, consecration, or repentance. They may not sound as theologically profound as *unregenerate nature.* But do consider them.

The underlying illness of the modern church is *false*

perception. In other words ("Give it to me straight, Doc!"), most Christians seem to be sleepwalking: walking amid reality but responding to an illusion.

Illusions?

Perception?

Perhaps you find yourself thinking, *Well, those other guys may be all wrong, but they certainly sound more biblical than this.*

Odd you should think that. Actually, nothing is more common to Scripture than the concept of perception. How, after all, do we come to inherit the riches of eternal life?

God calls us, we respond in faith, and he *reckons us righteous.* Consequently, we are able to forfeit our wages of eternal death not because we achieve righteousness but because God perceives us as righteous.

Through the sacrifice of Christ Jesus, God somehow comes to see the elect as perfect. Even after conversion we continue to see ourselves as sinners. So which is real: our perception of our sinfulness or God's perception of our perfection?

If we are correct, God is just a prejudiced old adoptive spirit and Christ suffered for nothing more than appearance's sake. But if God is correct—and how can an omniscient being be otherwise?—Christ has wrought something wondrous and real which many believers don't even realize.

A favorite Bible story recounts Peter's walk across a choppy sea to meet Christ. After a few steps away from the boat, Peter suddenly noticed the size of the waves and began to sink below the surface. One moment he stood with confidence atop the waves. The next found him demoralized and sputtering. What changed?

Did the sea change? Was it frozen solid at first? Did God perform a miracle and suddenly melt it, allowing Peter to fall through? No.

Did Peter's weight fluctuate? Did Christ miraculously rearrange the apostle's cells for a moment of instruction only to suddenly return them to the heaviness of flesh? Hardly.

Did God change? Was he in the mood for a miracle one moment and out of the mood the next? Not likely.

What changed? Was it Peter's faith? Is faith so tenuous and fleeting that it can be present in a wonder-working way one second only to dissipate the next? Again, the answer must be in the negative.

While everything else in the situation remained the same, Peter's perception changed. He began his walk in confidence, focusing on the sovereignty of God by looking at Christ. Only when he turned to look at the waves, perceiving his circumstances through the eyes of natural man, did Peter begin to flounder and sink.

In one instant Peter responded to reality, a reality which included the supernatural power of God. Later he responded to an illusion, a more rational perception which excluded God's supernature, and he found himself blowing bubbles.

Perception. It is nothing less than one of the distinctives of the Christian faith. Why else would Paul have written, "For we walk by faith, not by sight"? (2 Cor. 5:7).

For what other reason might Christ have said, "You shall know the truth and the truth shall make you free"

14

(John 8:32, NASB)? Notice that Jesus didn't say that his followers would achieve liberation through anything they might do. Prior to any action, simply realizing the truth would free them.

Knowing the truth would give Christ's followers the freedom to walk confidently through the universe. And in walking they would be guided not by their own sensory perceptions of reality but by God's revelation of reality. Is this not what Paul was saying?

Ours is a sensual generation. Not unlike Thomas in his infamous moment of doubt, we are obsessed with touching, tasting, smelling, seeing, and hearing. Because we pride ourselves in our intelligence, we choose so often to personally deduce what is real or what is artificial, what is true or what is false. We are inclined to trust our good judgment exclusively.

Unfortunately, even our very best judgment is often flawed and superficial. Because we are finite creatures, limited and short-lived, we see only fragments rather than the total picture. Our eyes can only observe so much. Our hands cannot reach beyond certain physical limits. Our reasoning ability, however immeasurable by human standards, is severely limited by an incomplete set of facts.

Consequently, man is easily deceived.

The average person is totally captivated by a good magic show. In the course of ninety minutes a sinister-looking fellow in his strange garb astounds us with amazing feats of "the supernatural." He produces parakeets from a hat, scarves from thin air, and flowers from those very scarves. He causes bird cages, cards, and boxes to vanish. And then, for a dazzling finish, he saws his lovely assistant in half and restores her, levitates her four feet above the stage, and then escapes from a tank of water sealed in a case which six members of the audience have certified as inescapable.

The professional magician generally acknowledges that he deals only in illusions. He confesses to being little more than an ordinary guy who depends on speed, flexibility, distraction, and showmanship. But using only those well-honed but rather ordinary traits, he seems to break all the laws of physics and biology.

In reality most magic tricks are disappointingly simple. Audience members are baffled chiefly through their reliance on senses which cannot gather all the facts.

Magic is the simplest form of deception. And though it relies on misinformation, it remains a sort of wholesome pursuit ordinarily devoted to diversion and entertainment. Even as they watch in amazement, members of the audience are very conscious of the fact that what they are seeing is an illusion. It has even been billed as such.

Other forms of deception are equally ingenious but less honest. Some grocers discreetly place pink lights above their meat counters to make brown beef appear redder and fresher. Others actually use manufactured aerosols to create a "fresh-bread smell" in their bakeries.

Advertisers recruit honest-looking, sincere-seeming actors and actresses to vouch for the effectiveness of one product over another. Sex symbols promise that a brand of toothpaste, a scented shampoo, a particular breathmint, or an expensive model automobile will make one sexier—more popular. Yet ten years of consumerism later the plain people are still fairly plain, and the unsexy people are still looking toward their next purchase.

The average American is surrounded by the illusory and the deceptive. Advertising, entertainment, and even journalism are all subject to distortion, misinterpretation, and outright misrepresentation.

But the most authentic, convincing, pervasive, and deadly illusions of all are not the products of Madison Avenue. Neither are these contrived by overzealous newsmen or ambitious politicians.

No, the most deadly and insidious illusions of all are crafted by Satan. They involve ideas and attitudes about God, power, pleasure, rights, life, and death—often determining whether we rely upon God or ourselves. So authentic are these illusions on the surface that they are accepted as reality, both widely and without question. So pervasive are they that we are all found walking among them every day.

Unregenerate men and women (At last! One of those impressive theological words!) have no means of discerning the true from the illusory. They are left totally to their senses, their logic, and perhaps the counsel of wiser but equally finite beings.

That's why time and time again the Bible refers to such people as blind. In so characterizing them, God is resorting neither to insult nor analogy. Limited only to natural eyes and natural reason, they are incapable of penetrating the illusory to comprehend the real. Without God's principles, no view of reality can be complete.

Like the mythical blind men who went to see an elephant but came away with four conflicting descriptions—

all wrong—people without Christ have fragmented, incomplete, deluded, and consequentially untrue perceptions of what is real. God calls them blind.

The redeemed are different. In his infinite wisdom, God has provided each of his adopted children with special "translating equipment." He has provided the Holy Spirit in conjunction with the Holy Bible to enable believers to see beyond the deceptive elements of life in order to latch on to truth (to walk by faith and not by sight).

That is why it's inexcusable when Christians continue to operate according to deluded, carnal sensibilities, responding to elements of satanic untruth. And if twentieth-century Christians often seem powerless, convictionless, and generally indistinct from the rest of the world, this must be the reason. *We are walking by sight.* We are deceived in spite of the glorious liberating truth revealed to us by God through Christ.

Why do many Christians conform to the world? Because they continue to see things in a worldly light. Why are they not transformed by the Word of God? Because they too often spiritualize it, compartmentalize it, or otherwise sterilize it until it seems totally powerless and without relevance. In other words, they accept it as *spiritual truth* but not complete truth.

Therein lies one of Satan's most basic and potent deceptions. He convinces children of God that the spiritual is not always relevant.

To discover the overwhelming prevalence of this single deception one need only ask a few probing questions. Ask a Christian what he would do should someone slug him without just cause. Many believers no longer contend they should turn the other cheek. But should one turn the other cheek and again be struck, what then? Many believers could immediately justify laying the offender out.

Find a Christian undergoing even moderate personal difficulty and compassionately paraphrase Romans 8:28-29. The *beguiled* believer, whose number is legion, won't be in the mood for that. "Would you please give me a break?" you'll be asked.

Bible verses will be relevant once again when things take a turn for the better.

Ask very many halfway probing questions of a few average disciples of Christ; and, though you may find considerable respect for the authority of Scripture, you'll find less support for the complete relevance of such spiritual truth. Implicit among many Christians, perhaps even suppressed or unconscious, is the suspicion that while God may well work in all things to bring about good for those who love him, those in question may never realize their benefits from whatever it is he finally does.

There is a very touching, yet enigmatic, moment that occurs in John's narration of the death and resurrection of Lazarus (see John 11:1-44). Jesus arrived on the scene where Martha greeted him with a veiled rebuke.

"Lord, if you had been here, my brother would not have died," she sighed (v. 21). (In other words, "How could you be so late? It's all your fault! And to think that we considered you a special friend!")

Attempting to disguise her great disappointment, she continued but the context makes it clear she was rendering mere lip service.

19

"But even now I know that whatever You ask of God, God will give You." She recited it, just the way any good woman of faith should do at a time like this.

When Jesus replied, perhaps a bit routinely, that her brother would rise again, Martha was quick to diminish the relevance of this spiritual truth. "I know that he will rise again in the resurrection at the last day," she intoned (v. 24).

Such excitement! The Son of God had arrived at her brother's wake, and Martha was so excited that she sighed and walked away to tell her sister He'd come. Yawn.

Hearing of Christ's arrival, Mary ran excitedly out to meet him. Jesus approached the tomb and asked that the stone be rolled aside from the entrance.

But lest he become carried away with his spiritual sugar pills, Martha again felt compelled to awaken him to life's harsh, cold realities. "Jesus, he's been dead for four whole days. If you move that stone, you're gonna stink the place up."

Why was Mary excited while Martha was disquieted? Certainly their temperaments were different. But even more importantly, their perceptions were different. Martha was inclined to see only natural limitations while Mary was able to discern supernatural possibilities. Martha truly thought the spiritual dimension of life was important but mostly on special occasions and holy days. To Mary, however, the spiritual reality was the most vital reality. And Mary was proven correct.

The sleepwalking church of today seems stricken by an acute case of the *Martha Syndrome.* We are torn between an illusion we refuse to reject and a truth we hesitate to accept. The result is congregation after congregation of double-minded Christians.

The Epistle of James succinctly explains why such a body continually flounders without real success. "A double-minded man is unstable in all his ways," one reads in 1:8.

Unstable: believers wavering between worldliness and holiness.

Unstable: disciples too timid to evangelize, too selfish to minister, too busy to pray.

Unstable: forgiven sinners obsessed with the frailties of one pastor after another, never content to follow.

Unstable. What other word could better describe a group plagued by the problems we find in the church today? And why are we unstable?

Because we are double-minded. We profess to live by faith but we walk by sight. We respond to life not according to what God has told us about reality but according to what our senses and our reason tell us.

Sometimes reality breaks through in spite of our bent to the contrary. Shortly after the US Embassy in Iran was overtaken in 1979, Christmastime brought a rush of televised interviews with families of the hostages. Most responses were quite predictable and not surprisingly so. Some expressed the sadness that dominated the season for them. Still others expressed hope. But one mother of a hostage expressed a change in her values.

"I used to think that financial security and owning a nice home were the most important things in life. Now I

21

know they're not. This has taught me that my family is the most important thing."

What had changed in this courageous lady's life? Not the value of finances, not the inherent value of her family —only her perception of those things. However, that altered perception enabled her to see a new dimension of truth.

It is nothing short of awesome to imagine what might happen if Christians should begin to respond to reality more quickly and more often. What if when tragedy struck, more Christians consistently claimed God's promises about being with us and bringing about good? Insurance agents would suddenly be able to see two types of people: hopeless, addled, angry, frightened victims on the one hand, and Christians on the other. Doctors and nurses would be able continually to see the actual, tangible value of trusting Christ. Funeral directors might begin categorizing clients differently: rather than the haves and have-nots, the hopefuls and the hopeless.

Precisely what might happen is reflected in the story of a young Fort Lauderdale couple named Mark and Debbie. For seven months they had anxiously awaited the birth of their third child. The moment came early, there was a long delay in the delivery room, and then the doctor emerged with a grim visage. He explained that the child had been born alive but was grossly deformed, lacking several vital organs.

Mark and his wife had been thanking God for this child for quite some time. They had trusted God's wisdom and his sovereignty. They had anticipated God doing something special in their lives through this infant.

When a nurse rolled the incubator into the room, the tired young father gazed onto the tiny, misshapen form of his newborn. The child had no chance of survival and lacked even the physical distinctions of gender. But to the doctor's sheer amazement, Mark smiled affectionately and whispered, "There's my little blessing."

The child lived for thirty-six hours. It was sometime during that interim that the father prayed, asking for wisdom. "God, you are the potter and we are the clay," he acknowledged. "I know you've done this for a reason. Please let us know what your reason is and what we should learn from it."

The reply came within minutes. When asked what peculiar malady could cause a child to be born in such a fashion, a nurse replied, "It's a very rare condition that strikes only one of every 10,000 newborns. It's sometimes called the *Potter's Syndrome.*"

Some fifty friends, family members, and medical staffers were profoundly affected by the tiny child and the response of his parents. What might have been a time of great heaviness became a time of joy and renewal. This transformation came to pass because Christian parents dared to look beyond the illusions of the moment to perceive God's timeless truth.

How does one discover reality? If the believer is indeed equipped with some mysterious translating equipment, where are the directions for operation? How does it work?

That is the topic of this book. By the time we have concluded, you will have programmed your mind with a system of biblical principles. You will enjoy the ability to look through walls of deceit and barriers of demonic illusion. And in seeing beyond, you will enjoy the liberty that comes from walking and living in the truth.

Welcome . . . to the *real* world.

2. Through the Eyes of Faith

By now you've no doubt realized that life involves an unending chain of decisions. Some of them are so tiny and routine that one makes them unconsciously. A perfunctory twist of a knob determines that water splashed on a sleepy face will be cold rather than warm. Others of life's decisions are ongoing commitments made in advance. "I will go to work," an individual may program himself, "unless I feel physically ill."

Somewhere between those minor quibbles and the truly profound decisions of life—career, marriage, religion, etc. —lies that stream of day-to-day choices. What does one wear? How does one spend this Saturday? How much should be spent for an item?

A routine assessment of this phase of decision making may reveal something shocking and unpleasant about yourself. Analyze the basis for most of your decisions, the foundational criteria upon which your choices are structured. If you are like most people, you may find that your decision making centers on three basic pegs: convenience, finances, and schedule.

Consider your family conversations around the meal table. Perhaps father shares the mundane frustrations of his workaday job. Mother describes the annoying practices of the neighbors and the rude manner of grocery clerks and salespeople. Daughter outlines her plans for the next week, complete with wardrobe additions and accessories. And, of course, son has another list of activities waiting for his participation.

Heavy decisions: Should dad take the car in for major repairs this week? If he does what will mom do for transportation in the face of so many errands and shopping trips? Does daughter need the new dress, slacks, and shoes she has requested, and can she spend Friday night with Millie? Can son get his football helmet this week, may he sign up for Peewee Football, and will he be able to keep the lost dog no one has claimed for the last seven days?

Hmmm. Is it convenient? Can we afford it? Do we have the time to do it, get it, buy it, or arrange it?

One British writer has aptly noted that television should not be reviled for destroying the art of conversation. Conversation, he went on to explain, has become such a pale and uninteresting shadow of its former self that it can scarcely be called an art and certainly deserves to die. But having established that most families endure a dearth of scintillating table talk, what else might the previous example suggest?

One of the misfortunes of the Christian scenario as it appears at present is that the most important element of reality is totally ignored. The implication of much that passes for *Christian decision making* is that convenience, finances, and schedule are the overriding circumstances of life.

Where then does the supernatural fit in? Do we not trust

26

and worship a supernatural God? Does he not promise supernatural intervention in our lives? Has he not suggested, and very strongly, that supernatural wisdom is far superior to worldly wisdom?

To observe the average Christian, one would conclude that the natural realm is the only sphere of existence. In spite of all the otherworldly talk sometimes found emanating from spiritual services, the most commonplace Christian life speaks volumes to the contrary.

"Trust what you can see, touch, smell, taste, and hear," says the typical Christian life. "Live sensually. Survive only on the basis of the natural: natural laws, natural phenomena, natural inclinations, natural expectations."

It would seem that many, many believers have either forgotten or totally discounted a fundamental biblical principle: *the supernatural is natural to God!* That is to say, the extraordinary is rather ordinary in the realm of God's kingdom. That *is* roughly the basis of that divine trait commonly called omnipotence.

"Why of course I believe that," many would argue wrongly. "I believe God can do anything! I believe in miracles! Why else would I have prayed for my Aunt June when she was dying of cancer? When my daughter ran away from home for several weeks, I prayed continuously for God to bring her back. When my wife was plagued by problems she couldn't talk about, I prayed for God to help her. Why else would I have prayed in this way if I didn't believe God could do miracles?"

The inarguable truth is that those particular prayers, as well as an innumerable multitude of others, stem not from great faith but from *great helplessness.* When science falters, medicine surrenders, politics fail, and money is insufficient: *pray, brother, pray!* Too often prayer is the night shift that comes on duty only after hope has punched out and gone home.

If such prayer—desperate and last in line—can prevent a hopeless person from being snagged on the reefs of despair, then it may well be worthwhile. But there is nothing noble—indeed, nothing spiritual—inherent in choosing to pray when the only other option is doing nothing. Even an atheist may pause to pray when there's nothing else to do.

Believers (and there's a reason we're called that) should be found in prayer long before that point. In prayer one essentially reaffirms the reality of the supernatural and summons the force of that reality to the forefront of a given situation. In other words, prayer involves taking hold of real power already available. It involves the denial of satanic delusions that seek to deceive and discourage.

Prayer springs forth from the fountain of faith. Consequently, it should be evidenced even in life's routine decisions. Even those trivial decisions made during the course of mealtime conversations ought to reflect some degree of faith.

"Whatsoever is not of faith is sin," Paul noted in Romans 14:23.

Aside from implications of faith in decisions, real matters of faith ought to further pervade those conversations. Unbelievers may well spend their intimate family times in discussions of material desires, whims, annoyances, and gossip. They may choose to watch television more and respond to one another less. Their principles and beliefs are not necessarily violated by such choices.

Christians, on the other hand, might well be expected to behave differently. Family is a priority among Christians, or should be. Likewise clean living and chaste behavior are essential. Compassion and understanding are crucial. If such principles and values are not at least reflected or implied in a family's most intimate time of the day, where else will they be found?

If this generation of Christians is deceived about reality and ignorant of the existing inability to decode it, it is because the last generation failed to teach these values. It is because mealtimes were devoted to small talk and preaching times were devoted to poetry and positivism. Behind all the admonitions to witness, pray, worship, and abstain lay a foundational principle to which few were pointed: *respond to truth, not illusions.*

Too often those other virtues of prayer, abstinence, obedience, and worship have seemed ethereal, ungrounded, and/or cumbersome. They have sometimes seemed senseless and without purpose because the circumstance that makes them all essential has gone without saying. Even today such virtues sometimes seem unnatural because they demand that we act in opposition to our natural inclinations.

Virtue seems unnatural, as it happens, because it is unnatural. But it is not *unrealistic.* Instead, obedience to biblical principles enables one to reach beyond the realm of the sensory/logical and all its uncertainty to respond to truth. Likewise, prayer enables the believer to transcend natural circumstances and the despair that seems reasonable in order to summon supernatural power from heavenly reserves.

Those biblically prescribed practices which sometimes seem so antiquated enable us to escape the merely natural realm where feelings can distract and deceive us, to walk among the totality of both nature and supernature. Is it any wonder that natural bodies and natural inclinations encourage us to abstain from those "antiquated and irrelevant" traditions?

Reality! We perceive it through the eyes of a divinely sensitized consciousness programmed with biblical truths. And both elements, the sensitizing and the programming, are crucial to the schematic diagram.

I would daresay that this "programming" is the most important reason for reading the Bible. Certainly there are occasions when opening the Bible may reveal a specific answer to a specific question on a specific day. Similarly, a few moments spent in Psalms may provide much solace in the wake of difficulty. But of vastly greater import is the act of opening oneself to absorb biblical principles, insights, and truths.

Time spent in the Word is not comparable to other reading. Scripture teaches that the Word is more than a group of words or writings; it is a force, an entity. It was present prior to creation. It became Jesus the Nazarene. It is all-powerful and we are exposed to it each time we open the Bible. Bible study is, consequently, not so much an act of study as it is an act of fellowship.

Through this particular fellowship one is impressed by the vast chasm between reality as the world sees it and reality as it is, as it was created by God.

There should be little doubt about whom to trust. Should it become necessary that you personally defuse a bomb, would you prefer directions from a bombing victim or from the individual who planted the bomb? In removing a stain from an antique sofa, would you prefer suggestions from the child who spilled the ink or the chemist who made it? In perceiving truth we must not merely trust our hunches and those of our fellow strugglers but, rather, the word of the one who created all truth.

So believers trust God. We trust reality to be exactly the way he says it is, despite appearances that may suggest the contrary. We come to recognize reality as the Holy Spirit enlightens us by calling to mind statements and principles mentally indexed and filed through months and years of Bible reading.

Sometimes it seems one could almost respond correctly to reality by behaving exactly opposite from the way demanded by natural inclinations. There can be no doubt that such is taught on many occasions in Scripture. Consider a random sampling of examples.

Contemporaries often tell us that life is a mere series of random occurrences. With the exception of a system of scientific truths or laws, they say, the universe is one of disorder and chance. *The Bible teaches that an omnipotent being is in control (Gen. 1; Rom. 8:28).*

Scripture makes it plain that humility is a key virtue and that the humble will find success and exaltation. The world believes that one wins through aggression, looking out for oneself, and intimidating others.

The average unbeliever holds that happiness involves the accumulation of possessions and the amassing of great personal wealth. *God says happier are they who give sacrifically.*

Our world is caught up in an obsession for independence. Men of the world, as well as their corresponding women, asserts that one achieves real success when he needs no one. *Scripture preaches that freedom lies in proper submission.*

Unbelievers expect to find fulfillment and satisfaction in the pleasures of sin. *Christians understand that sin promises infinitely more than it can deliver.*

Science suggests that we can find Utopia through the accumulation of knowledge and its correct application. *God's Word insists that man's wisdom is foolishness and that perfection comes only through applied faith.*

People of this world put a priority on rights: civil, consumer, personal, and inalienable (not to mention right-of-way) *People of God are taught to focus on responsibilities.*

The preceding is only the beginning, the tip of the iceberg, if you will. Yet already the most drastic sort of divergence has come to be demonstrated between the church and the world.

C. S. Lewis noted this ultimate polarization sometime ago when he wrote *The Case for Christianity.* Therein he proposed that should one encounter two distinct groups of people, each of which held a view of life completely opposite to the other, one would logically expect one group to fare rather well and the other to do quite badly. That is to say, the group which viewed life most appropriately would generally respond in the correct manner in order to reap the benefits of that life. The opposite group responding in a completely contradictory manner would logically be expected to meet with continual frustration and failure, their responses being inappropriate and their view of life false.

Lewis went on to explain that such is precisely the case of the church and the world. The godly give credence to one system of thought, principles, and perspective. The ungodly perceive life in a way completely opposite. But in the problematic upshot of it all both groups seem to be doing rather badly, both only muddling through. Why?

The most evident conclusion to be drawn is that one group is not living according to their convictions. This certainly cannot be said of the worldly faction. To the contrary, many seem to be living their selfish, materialistic, amoral principles to the hilt.

Hence the next most evident conclusion is that the church, the believing faction, is living in violation of stated principles. We too seem to have adopted the world's agenda. We appear to value the natural above the supernatural, the rational above the spiritual. We have been deceived.

Having arrived at that presupposition, it now remains for the Christian to adjust his perspective. The task of attuning oneself to truth rather than illusion must be addressed, and quickly. But how? Again the questions may arise, "What really is perspective?" "How does one go about adjusting to it?"

Both answers are simple ones. Perspective is the framework through which you see life. It colors everything you experience. Perspective might well be termed a "built-in prejudice."

By way of illustration, consider the likely attitudes of two imaginary inmates within the confines of the same prison. Imagine both having similar traits, similar interests, similar experiences, and comparable families awaiting them on the outside. Now add yet one other factor.

Inmate #12 has only one month left to serve while inmate #13 is in for life. How might their attitudes and behavior differ?

Inmate #13, ever mindful of his life sentence, will probably put a high priority on prison conditions. They're his reality. Prison rules, on the other hand, will have little value to him, conceived as they are by the outside world. Rather, he will operate according to the rules of survival, doing whatever is required to survive, protect himself, and fulfill his desires. Frustrated by a sharply limited existence, he is more likely to explode when angered, to fight when threatened, and to crumble in the face of impending crises. He is a lifer.

A mere month left of his sentence, inmate #12 is playing a dramatically different ball game despite the crumbling cellblock he shares with #13. His inauspicious surroundings and their deteriorating condition have less bearing on him because something much nicer lies just beyond them in the very near future. He needs to endure these surroundings only thirty more days before being set free.

Grateful for his approaching release he is more likely to obey the rules of society realizing, as he does, that his fellow inmates have little to offer him now. Because something better awaits him, he is much more likely to behave in a thoughtful, caring manner toward his cell mates inasmuch as they will still be here suffering long after he has gone on to a new life. Spurred on by the hope of what lies ahead, #12 is less likely to explode in rage, more likely to avoid a fight, and more likely to bear up under difficulty during these fleeting thirty days. He is awaiting release!

Differing in only one way, two imaginary men are immediately expected to manifest radically different behavior. Of course the differentiating factor underlying their responses is perspective. Each man's view of everything around him, and consequently his ensuing response, is colored by that perspective. One's perspective is that of a lifer, a man presently in the midst of everything he will ever possess or enjoy. The other's perspective is one of hope, anticipation of that which is to come. And what a divergence!

The unbelieving members of this generation are not dissimilar to inmate #13. They are here, so they suppose, for life. The world as they perceive it is all there is. That means that it must be comfortable here, it must be happy, it should be fair, and it ought to be acceptable. The fact that nothing else is expected tends to place a higher premium on the little that is here.

Herein are spawned the quickly clichéd exhortations of our contemporaries such as "Do your own thing!" If one may go around only once, it is essential that he find some "gusto" in the going 'round. When rules of morality or principle don't seem to square with personal desires, modify or scrap the rules. Make it. Do it. Enjoy it while you may.

The church, on the other hand, should be much more comparable to inmate #12. We are not here in this fleshly tabernacle for long for we are truly citizens of another place. We are heaven bound where we are scheduled to

rive any day and spend eternity. Not only is this life not
ll there is, but it's not even a preview. Indeed, it compares
o what awaits us only in the way a grain of sand compares
to a lush tropical beach.

The believer is called to exhibit an eternal perspective.
Herein lies the first step in adjusting an incorrect perspective. So take your mortal perspective and *make it eternal.*

I have concluded that this new drastically-transformed
perspective, the eternal one, accounts for the instant transformation of many new converts to the Christian faith.
After all, the immediacy of change cannot be attributed to
the incoming of the Holy Spirit because that happens to
all new converts, yet all are not so instantly changed.
Neither can it be the release of guilt; for, once again, such
is the immediate experience of all new believers, yet all do
not exhibit such transformation.

Though filled with the Spirit and released from guilt,
not all new believers realize the importance of an eternal
perspective. Some are converted with little familiarity
with Scripture. Others are not well taught. There must be
a host of reasons, but only some new converts are immediately able to realize the astounding implications of the new
perspective they have just been given through Christ.

Granted, becoming a Christian doesn't immediately
solve all of one's problems, but the accompanying perspective of eternity certainly renders those problems infinitely
smaller. Compared to eternal paradise, lovers' spats, family quarrels, financial deficits, and personal insecurities
seem horrendously small.

Yet beyond those paltry problems, the Christian perspective changes everything about one's life. The believer

is freed to act, think, speak, and live in a different way. Even before he begins to change, his world has undergone a change of the greatest magnitude because his way of seeing it has changed. Suddenly the new Christian is capable of seeing through Satan's translucent lies and illusions in order to discover the reality that has been there all along. For the first time, the new believer sees the world as it really is.

3. "Straight Licks with Crooked Sticks"

Good things need not always taste or feel good. In spite of all the joy babies bring to their parents and friends, their arrival is generally accompanied by nothing short of agony. A surgery which happily removes a malignancy forever may prove intensely uncomfortable in the short term. Friends can become much closer after undergoing hardship or difficulty together. And many wonderfully effective medicines may leave a bitter taste in the mouth, even as they heal the rest of the body.

There is no reason to suppose that all spiritual blessings must appear in a burst of glory. Moses spent long years in a blistering desert before God could offer him the privilege of being a divine diplomat. Paul was struck down and blinded before his eyes were truly opened. So if it's not the case in the secular world and it's not the case in the Bible, why do Christians seem so puzzled when spiritual blessings are not initially pleasant? Inversely, why do we conclude that all spiritual things unpleasant must, of necessity, be from Satan?

Paul generally had two things to say about the unpleasant areas of the Christian life. First, he observed that present difficulties were without significance when compared to the unending splendor of eternity in heaven.

"For our light and momentary troubles are achieving for us an eternal glory that far outweighs them all," he explained in 2 Corinthians 4:17 (NIV).

Second, Paul understood that God makes difficulty *beneficial* to the believer.

"And he said unto me, My grace is sufficient for thee: for my strength is made perfect in weakness. Most gladly therefore will I glory in my infirmities, that the power of Christ may rest upon me" (2 Cor. 12:9).

In spite of Paul's clear teachings on the subject, not to mention the weight of other Scripture verses in this regard, the matter of Christian affliction remains a bane to the existence of many believers. We don't seem either able *or willing* to make the comparison or the step of faith to which Paul so often referred.

It's as though believers are still awaiting some new philosophic form to explain it all away. And it's not as though Christian writers haven't already tried. Instead, seemingly everyone who has ever written about anything else has also compiled a volume on the biblical view of suffering: how to conquer, cure, overcome, or just endure it. Yet the search for The Answer goes on.

In a preaching-lab course during my seminary career, I was continually amazed by the number of sermons on suffering the seminarians felt led to preach. In a class of twenty, in which each student delivered two sermons for evaluation, fully half of those homilies addressed pain and grief in the Christian life! Their need to preach these themes suggested to me the depth of despair that many of my fellow students were undergoing. The content of these messages further indicated to me that they didn't really accept what the Bible had to say about the matter.

If we can contentedly swallow bitter medicine and opt for *natural childbirth,* why can't Christians cope with the biblical material on difficulty? Why do we find God's Word so unclear or unsettling in this area?

Perhaps God puzzles us because we're at cross purposes with him. His method of achieving an end he desires is contrary to an end we desire in our lives. In other words, if God wants to build character into our lives, wonderful! But he mustn't use any sort of hardship to accomplish that because *we're* trying to build *convenience* into our lives.

This might well explain why the marketplace for Christian books is awash with shallow titles and superficial treatments of Scripture. Success! Sex Appeal!! Happiness! Wealth! Diets that are fun! Fashions for Worship! Mountaintop experiences! According to promotional hype and gimmickry, these are the things God wants in your life. *And if Christians weren't anxiously buying such titles, publishers wouldn't be turning them out in such quantities.*

Compared to the list of qualities prescribed by those books, Jesus Christ would seem a hopeless failure. If the current literary fad among Christians is valid, it means that Jesus himself had almost none of the qualities God wants to see in our lives. He certainly didn't enjoy all those wonderful sex techniques recently given such priority by a variety of writers and readers.

Inversely, compared to the list of qualities prescribed by the Bible, many of our more popular Christian books seem like failures. What *does* God want to see in our lives? Love.

41

Joy. Peace. Endurance. Gentleness. Goodness. Faith. Meekness. Self-control. Walking in the Spirit. Not desiring glory. Not provoking one another. Not envying one another (Gal. 5:22-26).

Scripture has promised us the desires of *our* hearts only when we *delight ourselves* in the Lord. On one hand this means that if we focus on God and are content in him, our desires will naturally reflect his values. On the other hand it means that the man whose heart desires a harem and continual feasting on a desert isle is not likely to get it, his delight obviously not being the Lord.

When we delight ourselves in the Lord we consequently delight in his purposes. Therein are our tribulations turned to joy.

"And we know that all things work together for good to them that love God," Paul's most famous verse reads (Rom. 8:28). But a crucial final clause is often ignored: "called according to his purpose."

His purpose.

Does this mean that the victory resulting from our difficulties must be interpreted in the light of God's purpose? Exactly.

If God should work through a particular tragedy to build endurance into someone's life, but that person doesn't want endurance, he'll be hard pressed to comprehend what good thing has come out of all his difficulties. Certainly endurance is a good thing, or God would not desire it for us. Nevertheless, the Christian not in tune with God's purpose may not be disposed to believe that.

Natural man doesn't want endurance—longsuffering— as the King James Version expresses it. The very need for endurance implies the likelihood of pain and difficulty. Secular man derives nothing from suffering: Why should he care to face it, stoically or otherwise?

The Christian, however, does indeed derive something precious from suffering. As a result, believers ought to be as distinctive in their approach to personal hardship as they are in their various stances against alcohol, gambling, or illicit sex. Who would deny that many evangelical Christians are against those vices? No one. A distinction has been clearly drawn. Again, how many Christians are truly *unlike* the rest of the world when trouble comes? Do you suppose that you strike your unsaved neighbors as *different* when sorrow arrives at your door?

Two unsettling possibilities come to mind whenever I consider this aversion to suffering among modern Christians. The first option is that we don't honestly want biblical virtues in our lives.

Inarguably, there *are* many attributes and virtues each of us would like to develop. Few of them seem to fit comfortably into the New Testament world view. We want to be savvy, in-the-know, but not actually wise in the sense that Solomon was wise. Most importantly, we want to be likable, lovable, and popular. None of us wish to be offensive, whether through dandruff, bad breath, or personal, ethical, and religious values.

In matters of appearance, there are various attributes we can affect through our choice of physical accessories. High fashion clothing can make us glamorous. Physical conditioning can make us attractive. Makeup and hairstyling can make us sensuous or the right posturing can make us sexy. We want to look successful, sexy, fit, youthful, fashionable, and likable. We want to be regarded as knowledgeable or informed. But who gets compliments for being patient, joyful, gentle, or meek? Has anyone ever asked another person out because he found her self-controlled and humble?

It may well be the case that Christians have tentatively set these virtues aside, hoping to adopt them later in old age.

This brings us to the second possible reason for our unwillingness to endure hardship. Perhaps we hope to develop important Christian traits in a less painful way. For example, there seems to be this widely held stereotype of a patient, smiling, all-suffering grandmotherly type who bakes cookies and knows just what to say at any given moment. She can settle a young couple's argument with a few homey words, show a neighbor how to make good coffee, or endure mistreatment at the hands of her selfish children until they someday mature and realize how they've taken her for granted.

So many of us assume that with age come wisdom, joy, patience, and all those other traits we read about in the Bible. Why *suffer* for that stuff when all we really need to do is wait for retirement?

Why indeed? In the first place, the fruits of the Spirit are not endemic to the human race. They do not naturally appear in some people at sixty-five as blossoms appear on fruit trees in the spring. In fact, the things God wants to build into our lives are, by and large, alien to the human personality.

In the second place, experience alone—even long years of it—is not sufficient to produce the traits of Galatians 5.

I've known hardened criminals who have a wider range of experiences at age thirty than most people chalk up in sixty years! Their experiences have certainly not promoted wisdom, meekness, or patience in these fellows. Similarly, there are millions of old people populating the globe who haven't a glimmer of Christian virtue. Old people, like young people, are generally inclined to be selfish, impatient, envious, and stubborn.

There is no easy, natural way to develop the fruits of the Spirit or the attributes of Christian character in one's life. Like the hunter who rises before dawn and sits in a cold swamp to shoot a duck, the athlete who punishes himself lifting weights five days a week to improve his physique, the secretary who suffers near malnutrition to keep her fabulous figure, the medical student who endures years of demanding study and financial sacrifice to become a doctor, like all these ordinary people who suffer routinely for temporal goals, *Christians ought to be willing to suffer for eternal goals.*

This means that personal difficulty is an opportunity. When hardship strikes, it portends total disaster only to the unbeliever. For the Christian, it presents a chance to respond in faith according to biblically stated principles.

"My brethren, count it all joy when you fall into various trials, knowing that the testing of your faith produces patience. But let patience have its perfect work, that you may be perfect and complete, lacking nothing" (Jas. 1:2-4).

James suggests that personal difficulty should be a time of joy. It doesn't mean that one is unspiritual or forsaken by God. Far from it. Personal trial demonstrates that God is at work in one's life, refining, shaping, and burnishing.

So you believe in an omnipotent, omniscient, and omnipresent God? You believe that men should stop trusting themselves and start trusting Jesus Christ for their salvation. Right? Well, if your God is so powerful, so knowing, so present, and so reliable for all eternity, why does your chin hit the ground every time a crisis registers more than 1.3 on the seismic scale of your life? Why do you grow so irritable and glum, expecting others to make a special effort to understand you?

"One day somebody is going to read this book and take it seriously," Leonard Ravenhill writes of the Bible, "and the rest of us are going to be embarrassed."

I suppose I shall never forget my first new car. I'd had secondhand automobiles before, but this little white Datsun was the first new car I'd ever owned. Oh! How I cared for it. I had kept it practically spotless and scratchless for almost eighteen months when I had my first collision. My car received a major dent in the front, and I escaped with nothing more than a broken heart.

For most of that evening, I couldn't bring myself to tell anyone. Finally, I told my roommate Scott who responded with a cheerful smile and an exhortation to "Count it all joy, brother!" I could have strangled that fanatic! I hadn't shared some transient, ephemeral spiritual qualm: I had told him about wrecking my new car! What an insensitive clod!

Less than four months later, Scott arrived at the apartment with a dour visage. The truth finally came out. He'd wrecked his auto. It was a used automobile but his first, and it was dented on the right front panel just as mine had been. It had been his fault and he was totally humiliated and frustrated.

I was deeply spiritual, of course. "Rejoice in the Lord alway: and again I say, Rejoice" (Phil. 4:4), I exulted. Then I further reminded him of Romans 8:28.

It never occurred to my roommate that in the same situation just months earlier he had recommended that I rejoice. It never occurred to either of us that our glum responses to petty problems seemed to discredit whole sections of the Bible we professed to cherish.

We and our contemporaries could speak glibly of Bible promises when everything was marvelous and promising. So what? Atheists can spout maxims and proverbs when their bank accounts are balanced and everyone is healthy.

Ancient Hebrews realized that there is something almost sacred about sorrow. Tears of mourning were sometimes collected in a bottle and saved (Ps. 56:8). Even today, it may be easily observed that times of despair most often give rise to profound thoughts and meaningful creativity.

Dr. W. A. Criswell, esteemed pastor of the First Baptist Church of Dallas, was once asked to consider an outstanding young man for a ministry position at his enormous church. The candidate had performed exceptionally well at seminary and seemed to have everything going for him. It was only after a personal interview that Dr. Criswell felt obligated to reject the young man's application. He later explained, "He hadn't suffered enough."

Tribulation is a spiritual vitamin designed by God for the whole man or woman. As a vitamin provides needed

47

nutrients and elements for the body, so tribulation nourishes and matures the soul. It purges the soul of artificial support systems and removes the tendency to rely on one's own energy and ability. Personal difficulty restores our perspective of God as the loving and all-powerful Lord that he is.

In hardship, we are further reminded of the fleeting nature of the things our world has encouraged us to cherish. Finances, fashion, and physical appearance may be devastated in a moment. Talents may be lost and friends may abandon us. All things temporal can be taken from us instantaneously, even though we worked long years to achieve them.

Shared sorrow is capable of creating a bond among humans that transcends all other externals and considerations. Time and time again, people attest to the rapport that is so quickly established among strangers sitting in hospital waiting areas outside emergency rooms and surgery wards. In sorrow, people realize that they are not islands but parts of the mainland.

Personal trial can be a tremendous boon to one's walk with God, but the blessing does not stem from mere endurance. Thousands of people have suffered extreme cruelty and gross deprivation only to come away bitter, suspicious, and disillusioned.

Instead, the Christian is nourished when he responds to trial with complete trust in God and total alignment with God's purposes. When this is true, one is able to reap real and lasting benefits which money cannot purchase, and time cannot produce.

Perfection is a favorite topic in Scripture, despite the

fact that the concept makes modern believers somewhat uncomfortable. Interestingly enough, the word is often used within the context of suffering.

It is fascinating that two of the most thorny areas of faith for modern believers—tribulation and perfection—are closely intertwined throughout Scripture. It would seem that, if believers are indeed unable to appreciate their completeness in Christ, it stems directly from the failure to appreciate also the benefits of God-given challenges.

The Book of Revelation was written primarily to comfort first-century Christians who were undergoing violent persecution. They were being savagely executed for merely professing the name of Jesus Christ. Many of them had never even known the traveling teacher-carpenter known as Jesus of Nazareth.

Needless to say, these people had troubling doubts and questions as they met in underground catacombs and used passwords and signs to initiate conversation on the street. Were they right in what they were doing? If Jesus was divine, why did he suffer the most humiliating form of death known to man? Why was this now happening to them if God loved them so much? Would things get better? What should they do?

What kind of comfort did they find in Revelation? Things will get worse before they get better. Ungodly men will continue to govern. Many of you will die violently and few will escape totally unscathed. John did not quote serene poems and well-worn platitudes. He didn't try to tone it down. Neither did he lie, hoping that ignorance might prove to be bliss.

Essentially, he said two things: *"Hold on to your faith,"*

and *"Remember that God is in control and has already won the war!"*

These admonitions remain potent tranquilizers for even a day such as ours. They do, however, bear limited value as mere words if not underscored by our lives.

Faith in an eternal, all-knowing, all-powerful God is the key to seeing the truth of personal difficulty and tragedy. The hopeless dimension of tribulation is nothing more than an illusion. In reality, personal difficulties should remind us of God's promises. They should sharpen our focus on eternity. Rather than times for doubt, moments of pain must become opportunities for enhanced faith.

Tribulation does not mean that God has forgotten about us. Nor does it mean he has lost control, even temporarily. Essentially, it suggests that God has given us a bad-tasting vitamin that will help restore our strength. The artist is again at his easel.

4. Who Knows?

Christians have oftentimes been labeled *anti-intellectu-al,* and not always unjustly. No doubt, most of us can call to mind one individual or group of individuals who have insisted "faith is enough" when what they meant was "ignorance is bliss." In fact, I'm convinced that the popular acceptance of Francis Schaeffer originally stemmed not so much from the fact that people *understood* him as from the fact that it was so reassuring to hear a thinking man espouse conservative Christianity.

I attended seminary despite warnings from certain local pastors and deacons that "seminary ruins good men!" (I'm still glad I went.) My greatest irritation with many believers is that they don't seem to think about the implications of their faith. I would even propose that considerable amounts of rational thought went into the concept and content of this very book.

When considered at the beginning, these sentiments serve to underscore one important point: *this writer is not about to assail or condemn human reason or sound logic.* I would never contend that faith and intellect are mutually exclusive.

I do, however, hold serious reservations about "reason"

in its current incarnation. For what used to be a careful process of objectivity, observation, and induction has become a sometime bent and malicious sort of creed.

Carl Sagan received popular acclaim for his book and television series, *Cosmos,* in which he purportedly used science as a tool for explaining why everything is. "The cosmos," he asserted in his introduction, "is everything that is or ever was or ever will be."

With that blanket statement, the celebrity scientist launched his imaginary tour of the universe, setting forth his own theories, opinions, and speculation with the same unquestioned certainty as, say, the law of gravity. With virtually no distinction between the proven and the merely hoped for, Sagan intertwined black holes, the structure of DNA, his personal conviction that higher life exists beyond earth, and his personal opinion that Christianity has always been a barrier against human progress. All this was presented under the canopy of cool, scientific objectivity.

As a whole, *Cosmos* comprised a very personal but not a very scientific statement about the universe. By its very nature limited to what can be examined and observed, science can neither rule out what has occurred in time immemorial nor unprecedented and spontaneous events in the immeasurable future. Yet throughout a book and television series which continually presented the Christian faith as an obstructionist myth, Sagan freely presented his own personal faith as objective, scientific reason.

Men like Dr. Sagan can take such license because it has generally become fashionable to discount Christianity. Some critics point to various wars which have been fought in the name of Christ. Others reject the faith because they identify it with attitudes of negativism, condemnation, and prejudice, which they've seen in some atypical fundamentalists. Yet another significant host of people reject Christianity because they assert that the Bible is irrelevant.

How ironic! The first group *objectively* dwells on a handful of misguided military confrontations at the sacrifice of an endless list of significant contributions made by the church. Public education, humane treatment of the emotionally disturbed, the abolition of slavery, and the changed perception of women from chattel to human beings—these sterling achievements and a thousand others may be traced directly to Jesus Christ.

The second group of *intellectuals* are keenly aware of a few historic or present day fire-eaters, whom they may or may not be able to specify. Yet they appear to have selectively forgotten that enormous host of scientists, physicians, day laborers, and even presidents whose Christian convictions were clearly demonstrated through compassion, sacrifice, and a concern for others. If one can overlook such contrasting evidence in the name of objectivity, what constitutes prejudice?

Members of the final group of critics, those who think the Bible is irrelevant, must be personally encountered to be truly appreciated. Ask such a person to name even two biblical principles which are no longer relevant. Ask him to summarize the main point of Scripture in a few sentences or inquire as to a few specific contradictions he's discovered.

Do this, and you'll generally find that most people who

discount the Bible have never even read it. What kind of intellectual rejects a major literary classic without even knowing what it says?

Strangely, many thinking people who claim to be totally unprejudiced with regard to race, creed, or nationality are extremely prejudiced against the Christian faith. Bob Dylan was rudely awakened to this when he announced his conversion to Christianity in 1980. (Recently, it seems he has moved back toward Judaism.) Suddenly, friends turned their backs on him. Music critics who had raved about his previous offerings found his new albums revolting, uninteresting, and without significance.

In his song *"Precious Angel,"* he addressed his "so-called friends" who had "fallen under a spell."

Celebrities who dabble in exotic Eastern religions or who sit at the feet of mysterious Indian gurus are very chic on televised talk shows. (Incidentally, those same popular gurus are considered quacks and charlatans in India, and Americans who fall under their influence are considered gullible.) Scientists and philosophers who profess rank atheism are accepted with praise and awe. Adherents of Yoga are quite fashionable. Christians, however, are not encouraged to talk about their strange fascination with fanaticism.

Christianity creates problems because it asserts absolutes in the midst of a society of relativists. In the face of increasingly prevalent situational ethics, the Bible says, "There is an end which seems right to man, but its end is the way of death" (Prov. 14:12).

The American scene was aptly characterized by a sociologist who appeared on the *Today* show sometime ago.

"It's not that people think the rules have changed," she explained to Jane Pauley. "Today they think *there are no rules.*" (*Today,* May 19, 1982)

The Bible further flies in the face of conventional wisdom in demanding monotheism—absolute allegiance to one God. To the natural twentieth-century American, it seems reasonable to tailor any sort of creed or philosophy to one's own interests or life-style. Why, Buddhism allows this. Likewise, adherents of other Eastern religions, est, and a number of other popular disciplines of the day may involve themselves in an eclectic cluster of beliefs and disciplines suited to their own whims.

Still, the God of Judeo-Christianity is absolute. "Thou shalt love the Lord thy God with all thy heart, and with all thy soul, and with all thy strength, and with all thy mind" (Luke 10:27).

It is of utmost importance that believers keep these considerations firmly in mind when confronting statements of natural science, history, psychology, or philosophy, made by worldly thinkers. We are not always provided conclusions drawn in an objective manner by unbiased researchers. To the contrary, we are often confronted with the sincere ideals and opinions of individuals with priorities at stake.

Research which rejects unpopular evidence in order to arrive at predesigned conclusions ceases to be evidence and borders on sorcery. Thought which sacrifices objectivity and openness in favor of prejudice may no longer be called reason but rather, rationalization. And herein lies the basic fallacy of much of today's popular wisdom: *popular it is, but wisdom it is not.*

"The fear of the Lord is the beginning of knowledge," we find in Proverbs 1:7.

On the most basic level, the fear of the Lord gives us a true perspective of how life really is. Things may seem to be natural or logical, but there's more. There's God; and *he* is the life force, the guiding power behind all that is. The reverence of him is a continual reminder to the truly wise that there is the natural, and then there is the supernatural.

Further, this knowledge and reverence of God serves to temper our thinking and keep the mind in check. The human mind otherwise evidences a tendency to exalt itself, a manifestation of which many pop scientists are prime examples.

In spite of all its potential, the mind is finite. Limited by access only to what can be tasted, touched, smelled, seen, and heard, the mind must work within the bounds of human experience. Even the single mind with access to all the recorded wisdom of collective humanity may draw only from what limited mortals were able to observe during the span of a few thousand years.

Such a mind has no access to all that preceded the historical record or anything unprecedented that awaits humanity in the future. That mind has no access to events concurrent with human beings but taking place in regions uninhabited and unobserved by them. It has no access to any event or element, the detection of which lies beyond the arena of man's five senses.

This overwhelming limitation of that versatile mind is further complicated by a presupposition of scientists themselves. If the human mind is the random result of original disorder, how can one rely so heavily upon its very orderliness?

Carl Sagan would have us believe that such a limited and disorderly mind can, on the one hand, virtually prove the existence of extraterrestrials we have never seen and of whom we have no irrefutable evidence. On the other hand, the existence of an invisible God who has manifested himself in human history and has transformed millions of lives should not even be considered by the mind.

Libertarians and situational ethicists would have us believe that the mind can override all factors of personal prejudice, desire, hunger, intoxication, doubt, and frustration in order to analyze the essentials of a moral situation and make a wise and fair moral choice. They would jettison all absolutes in homage to human freedom and the ability of the human mind.

In this situation, the mind has been granted free rein to establish preeminence. We are promised that the mind, unrestrained by *religious superstition,* can ultimately rid humanity of disease and deformity, racial prejudice, war, and inequity. In the absence of religion and traditional value systems, they would have us believe, the human mind can establish Utopia.

So the mind becomes god, science is its religion, and scientists become its high priests. Only the high priests have access to the holy of holies, the laboratory. Reason, biased and manipulative, becomes their manner of administration.

One is suddenly aware of a hilarious and yet tragically ironic state of affairs. Christians assert that the human mind is the creation of an eternal God, yet trust it exclusively only when it functions in accordance with his preestablished principles. Many scientists, at the other pole, insist that the mind is nothing more than the chance result of billions of years of random mutation in a transient cosmos, yet they *exalt* that chance organ to the level of a deity!

Though totally inappropriate for the role of God, a logical and analytical mind is certainly a gift of God. In calling on us to love him not only with heart, soul, and strength, but mind as well, God is scarcely prescribing mindless religion.

Had he not wished us to make decisions and consider implications, God could certainly have engineered a more direct and efficient manner of communication than a thick Book to be searched and pored over. The fact that such a Book is his chief source of modern communication, however, speaks volumes (pardon the unintended pun) about how God expects us to respond in faith.

God expects us to think. Reading is, after all, a basic thought process, even reading the Bible with enlightenment from the Holy Spirit. Similarly, God desires that our obedience be not blind, unthinking obedience but considered obedience.

Routine and unthinking sacrifice is unmistakably galling to God according to numerous passages in Kings and Isaiah. In the New Testament parable, the son who initially refuses a father's request but then reconsiders and obeys is vastly favored over the son who mindlessly acquiesces but then fails to follow through.

We may also safely assume that God intended meditation—not sermonics—to be the primary source of inspiration and edification. The current emphasis on the authoritative *pastor-teacher* figure may well be a true need fulfillment in many congregations, but I'm not so sure it squares with the priesthood of the believer.

As far as I can tell, the first scripturally-based sermon may well be Peter's stirring homily paraphrased in Acts 2:14-40. Should that be the case, one can safely assume that the written form of Scripture predates the first pulpit exposition by 1500 to 2000 years. Any oral form of Scripture would go back farther still. All things considered, this concept of "pastor-chef"—a figure largely responsible for the total nourishment of the flock—must be a fairly recent addition to the order of service.

While one would agree that Christ exhorted Peter to "Feed my sheep" (John 21:17), it is equally significant to the metaphor that a shepherd did not actually mow down the grass and stuff it into the mouths of sheep. Instead, a shepherd's role in feeding had more to do with the general location of food than with the mastication and digestion of grass. A mother pigeon might have been a better analogy if pastors are expected to eat, digest, and then regurgitate all the food for a nestling congregation.

A pastor well ought to be a man of the Word, but neither he nor his people should consider a sermon as "this week's ration." When the present pastor-teacher fad eventually abates, perhaps we'll see a new crop of *pastor-motivators:* men who'll motivate their members to study their Bibles at home and "feed themselves."

The Bible itself is evidence that God expects his people to think. We ought to think about his nature. We should give thought to things we do in obedience. We should give thought to his Word in order to be inspired, edified, and nourished. *Isn't that enough to trust our limited old minds for?* No, there's more.

"All scripture is given by inspiration of God, and is profitable for doctrine, for reproof, for correction, for instruction in righteousness. That the man of God may be perfect, throughly furnished unto all good works" (2 Tim. 3:16-17).

You may have noticed that word again—the one that oft makes evangelicals discomfited: *perfect* (complete). Paul wrote to Timothy that Scripture is given that one may be complete, thoroughly equipped unto all good works.

God being omniscient, he certainly must have known about everything in today's world, even as he inspired his Holy Bible centuries ago. He even knew how a Christian might best respond in every questionable situation. "Why then," one might logically inquire, "did he not inform those biblical writers about recreational drugs, suggestive motion pictures, mind-controlling cults, latchkey children, revealing fashions, and income tax loopholes?"

Inasmuch as God expects the Bible to make a believer complete for all good works, one might also infer that he expects us to use our reason in order to discover general biblical principles which relate to contemporary situations. Of course, the believer is enlightened by the Spirit as he or she studies, but much of the process relies on basic rational consideration of Scripture.

How does a particular character in the Bible respond to a particular situation? Does God commend it as a prudent response. What is the general principle underlying the character's action or decision? Finally, to which circumstances in my life may this principle be applied?

As vital and desirable as the Holy Spirit proves to be in Bible study, he was apparently never intended as a substitute for careful reading and sound reflection.

In a technological era wherein university training is commonplace and television zaps humanity with an endless barrage of information, Christians can ill afford to be ignoramuses. We should be as informed and conversant in matters of faith as our contemporaries are in the drug scene, the entertainment field, and the political arena.

We must not defer the responsibility of thinking to others, whether those people be secular scientists, worldly celebrities, or even our own well-meaning pastors and ministers. We dare not regress to the Dark Ages of Christian ignorance, no matter how soothing the promise may seem.

Not unlike fire, the human mind affords tremendous opportunity for both advance and destruction. Reason may be perverted by crafty individuals for the deception of the masses. The fact that logic may prove opposing points has been demonstrated in countless courtroom battles and letters to the editor.

Yet no one is so capable of sound reason as a believer because no one else is so capable of knowing what is true and what is real. Who else is as capable of creative thought as one attuned to the mind of the Creator?

This then could be the generation in which the church stops merely responding to provocation and competition and starts breaking new ground in ministry. Why must Christian television continually mimic the talk shows and soap operas (and now, old movies) of secular television? Why is our concept of a local church television ministry so often limited to a pastor preaching? Why must Christian music go on in the style of either traditional gospel or rock music? Are there no new forms to be originated?

Why must the going themes in Christian books so often be four or five years behind the secular market? If they get rich on diet books, we follow with a market glut of "God Wants You Skinny" books. If they make it big with sex manuals, we pop up five years later with a wave of "God Wants You to Know New Sex Techniques" books. *What this suggests is that Christians think just like non-Christians, only slower!*

With so many varieties of denominations, why are there so few varieties of worship? And why must a given congregation worship in the same style every week?

Do I know what my denomination believes doctrinally, or am I what I am because I was born that way? If I found out what we really believe, would I agree with it? Would the Bible support it?

Is there a ministry that would be more effective than a bus ministry or Vacation Bible School in our local community? Could it be that these people need some new ministry that no one else in the whole world is doing? What would that be?

I know what it takes for a quack to get national exposure in the mass media. What would it take for a sincere Christian to gain national attention for Christ in a meaningful way?

Am I truly committed to Christ? If not, what would be different in my life if I were?

WHO KNOWS?

This screwy world is badly in need of Christians with new ideas. If you're a Christian, don't whine that you don't have the mind for it. *The Bible says you have the mind of Christ.* Believe it. And for goodness sake, use it!

5. Last "Rights"

The obsession with personal rights seems peculiarly American. This is not to suggest that citizens of other nations do not enjoy or even relish their liberties, but what other nationality can approach Americans in their virtual fixation on rights? It must have begun with the Revolutionary War when we asserted once and for all that we expected our *inalienable rights*. In the years since, we've expanded our awareness to include civil rights, student rights, consumer rights, and right-of-way.

Protecting these rights has become big business. We've developed public defenders, consumer advocates, and a legion of bureaucratic agencies to insure what is rightfully ours. And our cars include horns as a standard feature in order to personally warn or rebuke those who would dare tread on our rights-of-way!

Many American Christians would even go so far as to insist that personal rights are *sacred*. They would, however, be unlikely to find biblical support for such a notion.

This is not to say that rights are unimportant. They are, after all, God-given. They are also priceless in the sense that countless thousands of young men and women have died in terrifying warfare to guard those rights. Indeed, modern Americans can give priority to personal rights only because so many fallen young Americans have given a higher priority to *personal responsibility.*

Responsibility, not rights, is sacred. Consequently, it is to that priority of responsibility that God commends his chosen people.

Jesus Christ was so responsible during his earthly ministry that the New Testament bears examples on virtually every page. He was burdened with complex responsibilities, not only as a man and an Israelite but as a teacher, spiritual leader, Son of God, and Savior! Yet even in the midst of such crushing duty, he left not one instance wherein he demanded his own personal rights.

Writing to the Philippians, Paul made a profound statement about this facet of Christ's being: "Who, being in the form of God, thought it not robbery to be equal with God: But made himself of no reputation, and took upon him the form of a servant, and was made in the likeness of men. And being found in fashion as a man, he humbled himself, and became obedient unto death, even the death of the cross" (Phil. 2:6-8).

Civil rights? The only way the Sanhedrin was ever able to bring Christ to trial was by way of trumped-up charges, legal improprieties, and bribed witnesses. Yet in the face of such flagrant abuse of human rights, Jesus issued no demands.

"He was led as a sheep to the slaughter," Luke writes in Acts 8:32, recycling a prophecy from Isaiah, "And like a lamb silent before its shearer, so he opened not his mouth."

Christ's strking example is only the foundation in a

towering column of biblical material on rights and responsibilities. Verse after verse points the believer to humility and meekness. Christ further went to great lengths in his Sermon on the Mount to encourage disciples to go beyond what was legally expected of them.

When slapped they should offer the other cheek. If requested to share a cloak, they should share the coat as well. When requested to carry a Roman soldier's gear for a mile, the believer should go an additional mile. The example of divine love was always more important than the mere acquisition of rights.

Paul took up this theme in addressing the matter of believers who were taking one another to court in civil matters. "Now therefore there is utterly a fault among you, because ye go to law one with another. *Why do ye not rather take wrong? Why do ye not rather suffer yourselves to be defrauded?*" (1 Cor. 6:7, author's italics).

The Old Testament bears up the remarkable story of David who suffered at the hands of the paranoid, depressive King Saul. Even though he had already been anointed by Samuel as Saul's successor and in spite of the fact that Saul continually sought to take his life, David persistently refused to lift his own hand against God's anointed. In spite of his own personal right to self-preservation, David was impressed to honor his responsibility to the man God had already placed on the throne.

This lesson of responsibility may be the most difficult and distasteful one for American Christians to adopt. Indeed, most of the rights we so vehemently demand have little or nothing to do with matters of life or death. More often than not they are petty matters of pride and convenience.

In 1980, two Catholic nuns received international media attention. Interestingly enough, both were named Teresa.

The first was Mother Teresa of Calcutta who won that year's Nobel Prize for Humanitarian Achievement. She was honored in response to her utterly sacrificial work among some of India's downtrodden masses: diseased beggars, lepers, and the hopelessly ill. Providing things as simple as food or a quiet place to die, she worked from dawn to dusk, owned only two garments of clothing, and consumed a diet consisting of the same simple morsels she fed her flock.

A few months later Pope John Paul II visited the United States, and a second Theresa stepped into the limelight. Kneeling before the Pope for a brief perfunctory blessing, she stood and called upon him to take action on behalf of the rights of women in the church.

The two images provided an awesome contrast. On one hand, a saintly lady in Calcutta has sacrificed even basic human comfort but has set an example which mirrors the concepts of Christ's Sermon on the Mount. On the other hand stands a lady with whom most of us could identify, demanding her right to recognition and a higher office.

We are prone to boast how wonderful it is to serve God in our free country, but inalienable rights are not necessary to serve God. It's difficult to imagine even a totalitarian regime closing down Mother Teresa's ministry in Calcutta. ("Who cares what somebody does with a bunch of lepers, derelicts, and basket cases?") But if they should try, it's not difficult to imagine her adapting her work to a prison camp or work camp. And should even that prove objectionable to ruling powers, who can revoke one's right to die as a Christian?

Tragically, we have been deceived into thinking that our rights are the most important things we possess. We have further complicated the tragedy by allowing legal aides and labor leaders to polarize us into militancy. Somebody is trying to snatch our freedom away. We must make demands! Take direct action! Protect our personal space! Go to court!

We have opted for independence. We are convinced that if we work hard enough and long enough, we can raise ourselves to higher echelons of life wherein we are dependent on fewer and fewer people. Americans walk out on good jobs because they can't agree with their bosses on basic procedures. They walk out of classes because they can't tolerate their professors. And they walk out of marriages and families because spouses and kids have proven too restrictive.

We have identified independence with happiness. We have done this in spite of this generation's opportunity to witness two of the most independent and yet unhappy men ever to achieve celebrity status. Both Howard Hughes and Elvis Presley accumulated enormous wealth and the ability to make most of their own decisions. Entire industries revolved around them. But ultimately, both felt totally *forced*—driven against their own wishes—to abandon the mainstream of human existence.

Meanwhile, back in the mainstream the parade of rights seekers has grown as colorful as it has long. Over one hundred years after the battles have ceased, the American Indians are still demanding rights. Twenty years after the Voting Rights Act, Blacks are still protesting. Their company has been joined by consumers, Spanish-Americans, homosexuals, prostitutes, Vietnam veterans, nonsmokers, and even virgins.

There is still no outcry for inalienable responsibility. Most Americans don't vote. Many try to pay as little tax as possible. Others don't want to defend their nation or see that nation honor its commitments in defense of loyal allies. Tragically, in most of these areas there is little to distinguish the believers from the nonbelievers. *Most of us have been deceived.*

For sickly Christians obsessed with rights, God prescribes responsibility. To those doomed to meet with frustration in their futile search for total independence, He recommends submission.

Mention that word, and some Christians immediately grow tense. *Submission?* "Why must women always be the ones to be dominated, and what kind of Victorian, chauvinistic sexist are you anyway?"

Submission actually involves considerably more than women. Rather, the Greek form most often used in the New Testament, as in Ephesians 5, enjoys a highly masculine history. It is an ancient military figure which originally suggested "lining oneself up under someone." It was used broadly throughout the New Testament.

Essentially, all Christians are to submit themselves to God. In calling Jesus Christ our Lord, we are thereby expected to trust his wisdom and his strength. True inde-

70

pendence is thereby precluded from the life of the Christian even before he reaches first base.

All Christians are further taught to submit to worldly governments. First Peter 2:13-15 is one of several key references which instruct the Christian in the ways of submissive citizenship. Both Christ and Paul emphasized that all governmental authority comes from God. And in the case of Paul, those teachings found in Romans may well have been penned during the bloody reign of the emperor Nero.

In speaking of slaves and masters, Paul and Peter set forth a principle which applies to modern employer-employee relationships. Christians should make the very finest employees because they should be the people most loyal to the boss. Further, Christians are to submit to the authority of their employers whether they believe the latter to be Christians or not. Similarly, the Christian employee who uses "witnessing" as a pretext for continual religious debate while on duty may feel spiritual, but he's certainly not behaving biblically (Eph. 6:5).

While youth may be trendy yet a while longer in twentieth-century America, God considers age more significant. (Everybody's been young, after all, but reaching old age is something of an achievement.) In his first epistle (4:5), Peter instructs younger believers to submit to elders.

There's never been much debate about whether or not the submission of wives is taught in the Bible. The ongoing debate rages around what to make of those teachings. But frankly, there's not much ammunition for one side in this discussion. Ephesians 5:22 is one of several references which instruct the wife to submit to her husband under

71

God. Balance is found not through trying to rationalize this away but through reading further. The passage goes on to teach that the husband should love his wife "as Christ also loved the Church" (v. 25). Truly, the husband's biblical role makes his wife's task of submission sound like a breeze.

There's more. Christians are also taught to demonstrate mutual submission to one another. Paul spoke of "Submitting yourselves one to another in the fear of God" (Eph. 5:21).

Some have insisted that something's amiss here amid all this submission. How can a wife submit to her husband while, simultaneously, he must submit to her inasmuch as both are Christians? Isn't this contradictory? Some writers have used this seeming contradiction as a rationale for discounting the submission of wife to husband.

Other areas of life won't bear out this charge of contradiction, however. When a policeman puts on his uniform he assumes a considerable amount of authority. At his direction, the ordinary citizen must submit and stop, whether housewife, restaurateur, or lawyer. Each must submit to the authority of the law officer. Nevertheless, when he walks into a local cafe for lunch, the policeman submits to the authority of that establishment's owner. He sits where he is shown, and he pays what is prescribed. If a sign says "No Smoking," he doesn't smoke. Back on the beat he is dispatched to a private residence. There, as a public servant, he submits to the authority of a taxpaying homemaker whose child is missing. When personal legal matters arise, he submits to the experience and legal expertise of a lawyer.

Amid a variety of planes, mutual submission goes on among various people with various roles. The question of whose authority is in order in a given circumstance is mutually agreed upon, almost instinctively. And in fulfilling their roles of submission and authority, those involved experience the sensation of liberty far more often than that of restriction. Not only order, but peace of mind comes through mutually recognized authority.

In applying this to the spiritual realm, we catch a glimpse of the divine purpose of the Heavenly Father. Contrary to the charges of critics, the church is not necessarily an institution of legalism and severe limitation. A blind person is not cruelly restricted when made aware of a nearby traffic light and its stop signal. A child is not unfairly hampered when trained to obey his parents against his own wishes.

It is only logical to recommend authority to individuals with specific limitations, either physical or intellectual. That fact is widely accepted among humans. What is less widely accepted is the biblical proposition that even the healthiest adults among us are not complete either. Completion or perfection (that word again) is something we attain through submission to the authority and wisdom of a complete God.

Our own ability to reason successfully is limited because our perception is limited. We are handicapped both by our comparatively insignificant life span and our dependence on five incomplete senses. We are finite and limited youngsters in an ancient universe we did not choose and cannot measure or explain.

We address that universe appropriately through faith in

and obedience to an unlimited God, the Creator of our universe. With that true perspective, the concept of true independence conjures images of an untrained sailor adrift on a stormy ocean without the benefit of a compass or oars. It bespeaks of nothing less than recklessness.

These matters having been set forth, it now remains only to consider their application. What difference will a responsibility-conscious Christian make in a rights-conscious world? How can Christians hope to succeed through submission when contemporaries are, in the words of a best-selling book, striving to *win through intimidation?*

First, consider the home. The average church member would scarcely recognize his or her household if each family member focused more on responsibilities rather than rights. Imagine no more arguments over rights of privacy, rights to choose friends, rights to the bathroom mirror, rights to the car keys, rights to watch a favorite TV show, rights to rest, etc., etc., *ad nauseam.*

Suppose that rather than quarreling, each family member focused on responsibility. Father realizes his responsibility to minister when he arrives home from work, despite the fact that he may be weary and hasn't read the paper. Mother fulfills her role of encouragement and restrains her desire to rant about her misfortunes of the day and how hard she's worked to clean the house three teenagers and a weary father have now strewn with clothes, books, and snack wrappers. Daughter accepts her responsibility to keep phone conversations brief and to cooperate in preparing the evening meal. Son submissively mows the lawn and represses his desire to criticize his sister's hair, telling her instead that she chose a nice outfit to wear today.

That sounds so foreign to most homes that it seems artificial. In practice, though, it would resolve most of those screaming bouts which in Christian homes seem so foreign to the Bible.

Next, consider the workplace. Any employer would cherish an employee who showed up regularly and on time, always offered encouragement and support, could be trusted not to twist a knife in the boss's back, and never stirred up dissension. A supervisor wants support people who make him look good by doing their jobs well. That is precisely the kind of employees God has called us to be.

On the social scene, nobody likes a person who conducts himself with a holier-than-thou attitude. Equally unpopular is the self-righteous individual whose quickness to condemn is only exceeded by his intolerance. Fortunately, neither characterization represents the healthy Christian.

Called to follow in the example of Christ, we should conduct ourselves in a way that reflects his confession, "I have come not to condemn but to seek and save" (see John 3:17, Luke 19:10). We must not confuse the disapproval of sin with the disapproval of the individual sinner. Certainly, one has a right to express his opinion about ungodly behavior, but for the believer this right is often overruled by the responsibility to demonstrate compassion for the ungodly person.

If the above is true, Christians well ought to be the most cherished people in any neighborhood. They should make the best neighbors, the best listeners, the most confidential counselors, the most cheerful visitors, the most thoughtful friends.

All this notwithstanding, there is yet another factor to which the happiness of submissive, responsible Christians may be attributed: *the blessing of God*. Not only do submission and responsibility allow us to respond appropriately to the real world, but they further tend to situate the believer at the very center of God's will. There is, of course, no better place to be.

6. The Pleasure Principle

Pleasure is a fleeting and difficult-to-define sensation. Sometimes it arrives when one least expects it, while on other occasions it may elude one's wholehearted pursuit. I can recall instances, for example, when a mere conversation with friends has proven exhilaratingly pleasant. On the other hand, I can also remember a long-awaited visit to historic Williamsburg, which I thought would never end.

As it happened, my first trip to Virginia took the form of a week-long missions tour in which I was one of five adult counselors with some forty teenagers. By day we assisted in an outdoor-type day camp working with hundreds of ghetto children. By night we bedded down in tents.

Not surprisingly, the teenagers participated in an unending series of pranks and schemes seemingly until dawn each morn. The weather was a further complication because our tents scarcely protected us from a hard freeze on two evenings and a deluge of rain on two other nights. By week's end, I had not only been kept awake nightly, frozen, soaked, and mosquito bitten, but had also been attacked by a "harmless" water snake, mauled by hyper-active children, and sunburned. I had also lost ten pounds.

An ardent history buff, I had anxiously looked forward to a chance to experience Williamsburg's historic charm. Needless to say, by the time that opportunity came at the end of our missions camp week, everything in that village looked gray and I felt sore. Our four-hour stay seemed to last a weekend!

Pleasure is more than a matter of circumstances, be it a sexual escapade or a trip to Switzerland. Enjoyment also hinges on a variety of other feelings and sensations ranging from fatigue and hunger to jealousy and insecurity. It is, in other words, easy to recognize but hard to forecast.

Because transience of pleasure is a universal circum-stance not restricted to camp counselors or religious au-thors—it makes an interesting comment on the current US scene. Here pleasure is not merely a sensation: it's an obsession. "If it feels good, do it," says the little maxim so widely assimilated by now as to be cliché.

It's scarcely shocking that Americans are turning in-creasingly to psychiatrists and "recreational drugs." How does one satisfactorily evaluate his life against something so nebulous as the pursuit of personal pleasure. The fellow whose purpose is to grow tomatoes has an external stan-dard for self-evaluation. Even on a gray day in December he can still look back to 6,000 successfully grown tomatoes. But for the hedonist, one day of hunger or rejection can overrule a decade of delightful decadence.

"Accept yourself," the neighborhood therapist may counsel. "Set more realistic and down-to-earth goals. Don't feel guilty about enjoying yourself."

But in a natural state of things in which even atheists long for some sort of immortality—literary, political, humanitarian, or at least the preservation of the family name through a son—merely achieving self-imposed goals isn't enough. Every man desires that in some way his life should make a difference. Whim gratification is unlikely to make such a difference beyond the day of one's death.

Hence, the ultimate result of a pleasure priority is *displeasure,* displeasure with oneself and displeasure on the part of God. To their misfortune, many US Christians and congregations have bought into just such a life-style. Nevertheless, the fact that such believers may be labeled hedonistic does not mean that, interchangeably, their priorities may be called "Christian." They are not.

This is not to say that Christianity is not a pleasant or, rather, *pleasurable* faith. Instead, God has designed the Christian life to be the most rewarding life-style on (or beyond) the earth. Granted, some congregations don't *look* like they're having fun, and some pastors undoubtedly eschew the use of the actual word *pleasure* because of its rather worldly, sexual connotation, but this seems more the result of sin than divine strategy.

Pleasure does seem to have fallen on hard times within the bounds of theology, despite its overwhelming acclaim by the world at large. As a word, it's been superseded by the "great time" preachers say their crowds are having. As a concept, it never receives the sermonic support of such topics as, say, evangelism, church attendance, or prayer.

Conversely, the old Christian standby *virtue* is rejected by secular pleasurists. In their domain, pleasure must necessarily involve vice, secrecy, ego-gratification, or sex. To

Hollywood filmmakers to whom sex is so engrossing that they must present it from every angle and perspective, marital sex is a total gross-out. Likewise, no character can ever do anything so wholesome as going hiking in the Rockies without ending his day with a camp fire and a joint.

Biblically speaking, pleasure and virtue are not mutually exclusive. Rather, God presents them as complementary components of a rare and personal gift for which he paid a staggering price. Christian virtue is not offered by God as a further restriction in a pain-filled world. Instead, he presents it as the way to successfully traverse a world damaged and complicated by sin.

As an integral part of eternal life, virtue is not an option for believers. "For we are his workmanship," Paul explained to the Ephesians (2:10), "created in Christ Jesus *unto good works, which God hath before ordained that we should walk in them"* (author's italics).

Paul pointed out two important dimensions of virtue—goodness or righteousness—if you will. First, he asserted that such is the very purpose of salvation. Christians are saved *unto* good works, not *by* good works, as he pointed out just two verses earlier. Virtue does not contribute to one's salvation but does most definitely result from it.

Why otherwise would God bother with choosing a species such as man and providing eternal life for members of that chosen group? He certainly didn't need the fellowship: there was fellowship among the Trinity long before Adam and Eve tracked through the Garden of Eden. And if eternal life is nothing more than some indirect way of populating heaven, how do the earth and God's concern for creation fit in?

It would seem that God has saved us that our behavior might produce the ongoing, healing influence of his character in his marred creation. Jesus referred to this effect as our being the "salt of the earth" (Matt. 5:13).

Not only is goodness the purpose of the Christian existence, but Paul also insisted that our good works have already been prepared or ordained by God *that we should walk in them.* What a fascinating reality! God is not instructing us to struggle, wrestle, and torture ourselves to achieve good works. He asks us only to walk with him, and the virtue develops naturally along the way according to a plan he has already charted out.

Nowhere is the provision of God more unmistakable than in the biblical treatment of righteousness. In the sphere of eternal righteousness, that which gains one entry into heaven, Scripture teaches that God grants one the whole package. When a person responds to Christ in faith, God immediately reckons or perceives that individual as eternally righteous.

In the second area of righteousness, that of deeds and character, we find that God has already laid those things out along our pathway. In submissively walking with him, we more or less stumble onto goodness a step at a time.

Though righteousness or virtue may not be achievable in totality in the believer's deeds and character, it should certainly *characterize* the life of the Christian—*any* Christian. It is the thing to which we are called and created.

In addition to building such good works into the Christian walk, the Almighty Father has further placed a warning system in the life of every Christian. Like a pressure gauge or heat-sensing device, this elementary spiritual system warns the believer of impending sin.

The operation and response are equally simple. Whenever one feels inclined to sin, to temporarily lay aside his virtue for whatever reason, this should be considered a warning signal. The intrusion of temptation means "Danger Ahead." If the inclination is the signal, what is the appropriate response?

When the gas gauge in one's auto veers to *E,* one automatically locates a gasoline pump. Should the panel indicate an overheating engine, a driver stops immediately and checks the radiator. Likewise, when Christians feel inclined to deliberately be less than God demands, they should either summon all their spiritual reserves in prayer or remove themselves from the tempting situation.

God plainly intends that our righteousness should depend on him. Unfortunately, he commonly discovers that his children are linking their righteousness or virtue to other people and situations.

Most of us could relate to the situation of Frieda, the committed Christian secretary who avoids vice like the plague. Because she has so scrupulously precluded the dangers and inconveniences of, say, smoking, she adamantly insists that other thoughtless slobs who care not for their own temples have no right to subject her to cigarette smoke and odor. In offices, theaters, restaurants, and airplanes Frieda feels completely justified in losing control and shouting at co-workers or strangers who dare light up in a nonsmoking area.

Regardless of the degree to which one sympathizes with

poor Frieda, the unfortunate truth is that her righteous-ness has been linked to how other people, even rank stran-gers, behave toward her. A raging heretic who could never force Frieda to renounce God in a three-day debate can provoke her to disobey God with a three-minute smoke.

Consider Jay, the charming young Christian who finally gets a date with a beauty he's long admired from afar. On their first evening together he begins to discover that many of her personal interests and wishes are completely coun-ter to his Christian convictions. Though his particular church prohibits alcoholic beverages, Jay gives in to please a lovely woman whom he admires. And in spite of a long-standing commitment to premarital chastity, he allows his romantic inclinations a bit more leeway this special evening. A beautiful woman, a special evening—another sincere believer has fallen after basing virtue on people and situations rather than upon God.

Much of what we do to compromise our Christian vir-tue is in response to the seductive nature of pleasure. After leading a comparatively exemplary life for months or years, it's terrifically easy to justify a brief fling that has come one's way totally unsolicited. "I deserve this once in my life," we say of a particular indulgence in question.

Or perhaps a family member or co-worker has been treating me snidely for weeks. Then he makes an unjustifi-ably cruel remark about someone else for whom I care. It would feel so marvelous to vent my spleen, to let this deserving clod feel the full impact of my justified wrath! And not only would the stormy scene be invigorating, but it would also release tension caused by other sources as well.

This willingness to violate ourselves in the interest of pleasure doesn't say as much about our commitment to Christ as it does about our perception of virtue. It may well be that the world has finally convinced the church to one degree or another that righteousness is no longer relevant.

Could it be that too many years of hearing "sinless perfection" renounced by well-meaning pastors and teachers have caused us to draw conclusions never intended? I suspect this is the case. Realizing that nobody but Christ has ever or could ever achieve total perfection in this life, we've down scaled virtue among our priorities.

We give first priority to worship and fellowship, things more likely to be achieved. Next in line comes Bible study. Later on, prayer or evangelism turns up on a rung of the ladder. Only down near the bottom, intertwined with an abandoned sign reading "perfection," do we discover the strata reserved for righteousness.

Needed in today's church is a renewed commitment to virtuous living, to life-style focused on the character of Christ. What is required is not new rules, restrictions, and prohibitions, but a collective commitment on the part of Christians to allow the Holy Spirit to elevate us above the compost heap of compromise, so acceptable to secular contemporaries.

We must conclude anew that unchaste and unholy conversation—whether obscenity, innuendo, or gossip—is unacceptable. Not only is such generally displeasing to God, but it specifically appeals to the flesh: the carnal man. We must realize that our abstinence from a certain

84

sin is abrogated when our conversation and behavior suggest that we are partakers.

The power of biblical meekness needs to be once again familiar to Christians. Ours is not a calling to level opponents with the fire of our rhetoric but rather to influence them with the force of Scripture and the strength of our God-given character. The Holy Spirit would seem much more free to work in the life of another if that person admires what God has already done in us.

Forgotten by too many of us are the vast benefits of righteous living. Enormous confidence may be derived from the assurance that, regardless of the unknowns and uncertainties that may await in a new situation, one has absolute certainties upon which to base a response.

On the more mundane, day-to-day level of living, virtuous people are easily trusted. Even people who don't agree with your principles will trust a consistently virtuous life, and innumerable opportunities for ministry arise. Scripture teaches that godly living enhances health and lengthens life.

Parents are likely to have less immoral rebellion from teenagers if biblical teachings have been expounded against a backdrop of righteous living.

Yet the most dramatic benefits are those coming directly from God when our lives are pleasing to him. And therein is found the true place of pleasure in the life of the believer. *Divine blessings bring pleasure into our lives when those same lives first bring pleasure unto God.*

Knowing that God calls for righteous living because it is beneficial, it isn't surprising to find sin prohibited because it is destructive. So great is its potential for devastation that Paul wrote, "I would have you wise unto that which is good, and simple [naive] concerning evil" (Rom. 16:19).

Of course, this flies into the face of contemporaries in a society where "knowledge is power." Everyone longs to be savvy, hip—to know *what's going on*. Code words and phrases arise only to be replaced by new slang, passed savvily along so that only insiders know the meaning, while users of those phrases can seem like insiders.

Snow, smack, chasing the dragon, S & M, AC/DC—the ultrahip tide of popular decadence continues to sweep the foundations of national morality. Subtle definitions are conveyed in self-consciously cryptic messages. Approval is conferred by popular acceptance of the term.

Sadly, even the Christian community often gets ensnared in the pretense. "By all means, we must be *aware!* We dare not be relegated to the realm of irrelevance through our ignorance of current fads and crazes." What's new in drugs? We insist upon knowing. What's happening in kinky sex? What are the stars doing in LA tonight?

Granted, we don't often participate or generally even approve, at least on the surface. Yet Christ suffers at the hands of our savvy. We're marked by it, coded into a world from which he's trying to transform us. Sometimes in our overcompensation to prove we're not shocked by a new twist in sin, we seem to condone it. So the borderline cases feel more secure in their deadly indulgence now that they've found Christians who approve.

So constant is the rapid innovation of the sin industry that the significance is often lost on critics as well as participants. Somewhere along the conveyor belt, someone must be asking the question *why?* If this stuff is so fulfilling and imminently pleasurable, why the constant flux: *new wrinkles, new positions, new procedures, new combinations, new names?*

The answer may be found in the Bible as early as the third chapter of Genesis. The familiar story deals with a couple, a serpent, a garden, a forbidden tree, and God. In the midst of perfection, Satan took the form of a serpent in order to subject the woman Eve to humanity's inaugural temptation.

Even a superficial reading of the passage reveals that the temptation took the form of two promises. When Eve explained that she should not touch the forbidden fruit lest she die, Satan promised, "You won't *really* die." Later, after Eve elaborated on God's warning, the serpent responded with a second promise, "That fruit will make you like God" (see Gen. 3:1-6).

This quaint story does more than qualify Adam and Eve as the first unfortunate victims of high-pressure sales tactics. It further establishes, and rather early on in Scripture, the reason for both sin's appeal and its devastation. That is, *sin always promises more than it can deliver!*

By the end of Genesis 3, Satan and Co. had achieved a 100 percent record for customer dissatisfaction. Neither of the highly alluring promises came to pass. First, the errant couple realized that they would indeed die, not simply mortally but eternally. Not only would they die, but they would die totally separated from the God who had been their Creator, Benefactor, and Friend. And second, the fruit had not made them like God. It had, in fact, made them less like God than they had been originally, for the disobedience had marred his image within them.

In addition to the failed promises of Satan, the couple suffered other untold horrors. Relationships were damaged, the soil was cursed, childbearing would become painful, and the character of their children would be so affected by this first disobedience that a son would be murdered by his brother. And that would be only the beginning!

Adam and Eve learned in a moment something that many enlightened Americans still refuse to admit: sin always promises more than it can deliver. It cannot come through with the joys and wonders it promises in advance. That explains why promiscuous sex must grow kinkier, why gossip grows juicier, why drugs must be taken in larger quantities and then combined, and why the porn industry has advanced from women to gays to children to animals to corpses.

Because sin cannot deliver, it must either hopelessly addict its prey as in the case of alcohol or heroin, or it must continually adapt its appeal. Satan has proven himself to be phenomenally adept at both ploys.

Into the midst of this moral quagmire of the United States beams at least one enormously promising ray of hope. With so much freedom to experiment in the gross variety of debauchery, there's also the enhanced possibility that many pleasure seekers might catch on at an earlier age and realize the hopeless emptiness of their indulgent lives.

If only Christians could be standing by to minister, not compromised and carnal but towering as examples of the transformed Christian life. Addicts and alley crawlers, prostitutes, and porn addicts could all look up from their despair and see truly distinctive people: *happy people,* biblical Christians.

"Religion that is pure and undefiled before God and the Father is this," wrote James (1:27, RSV), "to visit orphans and widows in their affliction, *and to keep oneself unstained from the world"* (author's italics).

Unstained by the world? Now there's a novel idea. Obviously God is ready for it, but are his people?

Envision sin as a steep, bottomless chasm full of darkness and danger, a favorite seminary professor once instructed our class. The closer one gets to the edge of that chasm, the harder it becomes to see. And the edge itself is terribly slippery and treacherous.

Now God has warned us that the chasm is deadly, and he has called his people to get as far away from it as possible. Unfortunately, today's Christians find that chasm of sin rather seductive. They try to walk as closely as possible to the edge without falling in.

As that beloved professor so wisely noted, God has called us to live as far distant from sin as possible. He has commissioned us to live unspotted by the world, to conduct our lives in virtue and righteousness.

The siren song of Satan should have no sway with believers. While Satan promises only moments or months of pleasure, moments he cannot bring to pass, God offers an eternity in heaven. His promises have never gone unfulfilled.

This means that we don't have to "go for it," as the popular phrase admonishes others. We don't need to grab for all the gusto or burn ourselves out furiously and passionately living for today. We are promised an eternity of unparalleled pleasure in the presence of the God who loves us with an intensity beyond any passion mortal man has ever known.

With that sort of exuberant tranquility waiting before us, how dare we lead lives like those who have no hope? How can we be so unwise as to settle for their standards, their hip phrases, and their cheap thrills which end in tawdry emptiness?

Until we can realize the splendors prepared for us by God in heaven may we strive to realize the good works prepared along our pathway as we walk with Christ. Our challenge is to show the watching world lives so untainted, so distinctive, that they must ask questions about us and about themselves.

In the admonition of Christ, our lights should so shine that men might see our good works and glorify our Father who is in heaven (Matt. 5:16). May this very thing be truly said of our generation!

7. The Cosmic Conflict

One of the great contradictions of human nature is the existence of humanity's bent for violence alongside its innate desire for peace. Even as wars and rumors of war perpetually simmer throughout the global stewpan, the chief elected and appointed representatives of humanity call out again and again for peace.

Asked not long ago by *TV Guide* to fantasize the story they'd most like to cover in the future, more television news reporters wanted a story about world peace. The greatest eulogy that can be given a fallen world leader is the benediction: "He was a man of peace." We even have a highly esteemed international award for peacemakers.

For the cause of peace, diplomats shuttle back and forth from nation to nation. Crowds rally with signs demanding that the United States and USSR simultaneously lay down their arms and establish a precedent of peace. We must all learn to cooperate, to settle for what is already ours, and to strive for harmony, certain idealists insist.

Strangely, many of the peace rallies and petitions of our day are either led or endorsed by celebrities from the entertainment world. Even as they suggest cooperation, treaties, and restrained ambition, many of these very celebrities refuse to "settle" for their present elevated status and unprecedently exorbitant salaries. Demanding still higher wages and more recognition, they break contracts, stall productions, walk out on strikes, and storm out of studios to be driven away in expensive cars to expensive mansions in spectacular locations.

There is the suggestion that somehow people will make sacrifices in the name of peace that they would not otherwise make in the interests of greed or lust. This premise unfortunately overlooks the reality that greed and lust enjoy a far more secure existence in today's world than either peace or, for that matter, charity.

Consequently, it is less than idealistic to expect the limitation of arms to achieve peace: *it is naive.* Before bombs and missiles, there were shooting wars. Before that, there were spears and swords. Prior to that, there were sticks and clubs. And before that, Cain apparently murdered his only brother with his bare hands.

The problem has less to do with weapons than with circumstances. *We are a fallen race living in the midst of a cosmic battlefield, and we don't know how to respond to the situation.*

In his critically acclaimed 1980 film *The Big Red One,* director Samuel Fuller used a realistic World War II scenario to demonstrate the absurdity of war. Perhaps the most telling image came from a Belgian insane asylum temporarily being shared by Nazi regulars.

It is mealtime, and the patients routinely shovel down their food, totally oblivious to the German troops sharing the dining hall. When a lady in red enters and begins to dance atop the tables the Germans watch leeringly, but the patients are unmoved. Then in a hail of gunfire a squad of US soldiers storms the dining hall, bodies flying left and right. In the midst of the deadly chaos, the patients continue to eat calmly. Finally, one of their number responds. Lifting a fallen machine gun, he leaps to his feet and begins to fire wildly, shouting all the time, "I'm like you! I'm sane! I'm sane!"

Not unlike Fuller's insane people, humanity is out of touch with reality. We've come to focus on the routine, the existential. We want to believe that the fighting is safely distant from us, but the great war has been raging in our very midst all along.

C. S. Lewis described a cosmic civil war being fought between God and Satan for the domination of the earth. He characterized the earth as "the dark planet," a place presently under satanic influence and out-of-line with God's plan. In Lewis's view, best described in his *Science Fiction Trilogy,* the earth had become a source of malignancy that spread prodigiously wherever earthlings were able to travel.

One might note that during Lewis's lifetime what we'd classify as "space technology" was still years away. Some time later manned flights into space would become a reality and the space race would heat up, but "solely for the peaceful exploration of space." As Lewis might have explained, however, human beings could not cast off their violent nature before speeding into space. Soon spy satellites were a reality. Now killer satellites are poised in space, capable of knocking out other satellites—and who knows what else?—out of action. The malignancy spreads.

Lewis's view was hardly novel. Rather, it was carefully cultivated from biblical teachings.

Advocates of a tranquil, pacifist Christ must grit their teeth when they read Christ's remarks in Luke 12:49-52. "I came to bring fire on the earth, and how I wish it were already kindled! . . . Do you suppose that I came to give peace on earth? I tell you, not at all, but rather division."

Paul used every opportunity to remind his disciples that theirs was a battlefield ministry. "Finally, be strong in the Lord," he wrote in Ephesians 6:10-12 (NIV), "and in his mighty power. Put on the full armor of God so that you can take your stand against the devil's schemes. For our struggle is not against flesh and blood, but against the rulers, against the authorities, against the powers of this dark world and against the spiritual forces of evil in the heavenly realms."

On at least two other occasions, Paul referred to one's spiritual resources as *weapons* or *armor.* In Romans 6:13, he warned believers not to use parts of their bodies as "instruments of unrighteousness."

So there's a war going on, we're told. Yet most of us sit languidly by, immersing ourselves in the mundane and wondering why life is so imponderable. The unbelieving masses can to one degree or another justify their behavior: they haven't read the Bible to learn this startling bit of news in the first place. Besides, they swallowed the secular line of thinking long ago. They believe anything disordered or problematic is the result of the random evolution of things over the last few centuries. No meaning.

But what about the Christians? Surely *we* have read the Bible. How could we seem so ignorant of what is going on?

Maybe some of us have adopted a secular worldview as well. Or perhaps we've just overreacted to the use of imagery in the Bible.

No intelligent person *actually* "takes the Bible completely literally" as some fire-eaters profess to do. That's because all of Scripture was not written to be taken literally. When one deals with spiritual or intangible concepts, it is often necessary to invoke various forms of imagery in order to do so. In this manner Christ referred to himself on various occasions as a vine, a door, and a shepherd. Yet no one really believes he was green with leaves or brown, or wooden, or rectangular with a handle. Instead we assume he was using metaphors to express spiritual realities.

Nobody really believes the kingdom of heaven is *exactly* like a lost penny or a net dragged out of the sea. To be sure the Bible describes it thus, but one automatically assumes the Bible is using simile to make a spiritual point. (It could grow rather tedious spending eternity in a damp, smelly fishnet, eh?)

For that reason, some believers may have read the numerous biblical references to spiritual warfare only to invalidate or devalue them as being metaphorical. *Spiritual* warfare? It did say spiritual, didn't it? That must just be symbolism for the ongoing contradiction between good values and evil values. Right?

Wrong.

Spiritual warfare is not one of those cases of poetic license. To the contrary, it is a painful reality reflected throughout the Bible. The first hint comes in the Eden narrative of Genesis as the serpent tempts Eve to disobey

God. We have to suppose that there's more to this than a mere devilish prank.

Later, we see God continually demand that the people of Israel *consecrate* themselves before undertaking his supernatural purpose. There's obviously more at stake in these cases than mere good conduct for the sake of good conduct. On other occasions we actually glimpse the divine forces as in 2 Kings 6 (NIV) when Elisha and a servant are surrounded by enemy troops.

"Don't be afraid," read the words of the prophet comforting his anxious servant. "Those who are with us are more than those who are with them."

Then the prophet prayed, and the servant's eyes were opened. He saw "the hills full of horses and chariots of fire all around Elisha."

In one of his first characterizations of his imminent church, Christ remarked that "the gates of hell shall not prevail against it" (Matt. 16:18). Nothing less than a clash of supernatural forces is denoted here.

"Then the end will come, when he hands over the kingdom to God the Father after he has destroyed all dominion, authority and power," Paul wrote of Christ (1 Cor. 15:24, NIV). "For he must reign until he has put all his enemies under his feet. The last enemy to be destroyed is death" (vv. 25-26).

Consistently throughout the Old Testament and the New, the weight of Scripture rests on the side of C. S. Lewis and like minds who point to a literal, ongoing war—both timeless and generally invisible. And while the Book of Revelation would assure us that the ultimate weapon has already been introduced (grace available through the work of Christ) and will eventually bring a victorious conclusion for the side of Christ, skirmishes do continue in the interim.

The person who accepts this premise might logically ask, "Who's fighting this war and how is it being fought?" One might puzzle over the nature of the weapons. Yet another crucial matter involves the stakes. What is being fought over here? Important answers may be found in 2 Corinthians 10:3 and following:

"For though we live in the world, we do not wage war as the world does. The weapons we fight with are not the weapons of the world. On the contrary, they have divine power to demolish strongholds. We demolish arguments and every pretension that sets itself up against the knowledge of God, and we take captive every thought to make it obedient to Christ."

Ours is a battle for the minds of men. We overcome arguments. We banish false pretensions. We seek to establish as our beachhead the knowledge of Christ. Thoughts are taken captive and subdued. The front lines of this battle may be found within the human mind, but that's not the prize. No, this is no supernatural popularity contest in which forces struggle to gain votes for God or Satan. There is more at stake here than popularity.

By winning the minds of men Satan is also able to win their souls. It is those souls that are the spoils of this eternal warfare. The victory for the forces of God is certain. Satan's banishment to hell along with his co-conspirators is, likewise, a sure thing. But prior to that "last shot," the skirmishes for territory—the human mind—go on. Undecided is not the outcome of the war, but the outcome for the souls of people like John and Mary Doe. Christ's victory will be meaningless for them if they are banished to hell afterwards.

As in other areas of theology, there are numerous phases of this spiritual warfare that we don't understand. Satan appearing before God to request permission to trouble one of the saints, as in the case of Job, is a concept that wholly mystifies us. Similarly, when Christ told Simon Peter, "Satan has asked to sift you as wheat" (Luke 22:31, NIV), the inquisitive Christian may be baffled. To my knowledge, this variety of interaction between combatants has no corresponding point of reference within the human experience. That is, we can't relate to it.

Other dimensions of the warfare seem more familiar. There is equipment and there are weapons. There is a strategy or battle plan. And, of course, there are casualties and prisoners of war.

The equipment is listed briefly in Ephesians 6 where Paul compares the weapons of spiritual warfare to those of earthly battle. The first weapon, truth, is compared to a belt in its function of holding everything together (v. 14). All that we do in spiritual warfare is based on truth. Hence, deceit can never be a weapon of Christian warfare. The end does not justify the means.

Righteousness is characterized as a breastplate (v. 14) which was important to ancient soldiers because it shielded the one area of the body containing most of the vital organs. Like a breastplate righteousness deflects slurs, insinuations, and objections to the gospel. The believer who has lived in a manner beyond reproach can confidently do battle, unafraid that lesser men may find that fatal chink in the armor and cut him to the heart.

Readiness is comparable to sturdy boots in that it enables the believer to cross any terrain to do battle (v. 15). The believer equipped with readiness is ever able to respond quickly to the prompting of the Spirit and follow wherever he bids.

Faith is like a shield in its function of deflecting doubts hurled against the Christian by Satan (v. 16). This is not to say that believers never have doubts but, rather, that faith disposes of them before they inflict a wound.

Notice the analogy for salvation. It is presented as a helmet (v. 17), that item which protects the head generally and the brain specifically. Salvation secures the mind and, consequently, the soul. Here again comes implicitly to the front that territory which this warfare is all about.

Only one weapon for offensive warfare—the sword of the Lord—is included in Paul's list. In the battle for the mind, persuasion is an unreliable weapon. Neither can force or coercion be relied upon to lead one to a sincere commitment to Christ Jesus. The weapon recommended by Paul is God's Word (v. 17).

The thrust of the New Testament suggests at least two other weapons. The more prominent of those would be one's own personal witness. On the most basic level, to bear witness means simply to verbalize what one has experienced. The apostles, for example, were glad to verbalize the things they had seen and heard, both during their ministry with Jesus of Nazareth and following his crucifixion and resurrection.

The second weapon suggested by Scripture is prayer. In

ancient days as well as on the modern scene, the finest weapon any nation can muster is a more powerful ally. Along those lines, prayer is the communication that puts us in touch with our ally, who happens to be the most powerful in the universe. The warring nation with any sense of strategy doesn't wait until defeat is nigh to link herself with a more powerful friend. Instead, she aligns herself with that more powerful friend from the outset. Neither does the shrewd Christian wait until all else has failed before calling upon God.

In spiritual warfare as in physical warfare, the effectiveness of any weapon is directly proportionate to the efficiency of the one operating it. For this reason, the US Army assigns a new recruit one rifle which he keeps throughout his training. It's called his "piece," and it becomes a part of him. The recruit handles the piece continually, disassembling and reassembling it. He cleans it. He conducts basic maintenance. He carries it twelve hours a day. When crossing rivers or streams his head may get wet, but his piece must stay dry.

Six months later in the heat of battle, the soldier knows he can rely on his rifle. He knows every inch of it—every mechanism. He understands things that could malfunction and how to remedy them. He can break it down and reassemble it in just seconds, blindfolded. Man and weapon have become a synchronized and deadly efficient fighting machine.

The spiritual warrior's proficiency with his basic weapons should be no less remarkable. But quite sadly, if believers had to rely on their own Bible familiarity in life and death situations, the majority would helplessly perish.

In a hopefully brief era of trivia mania wherein people program their brains with batting averages, television actors' birthdays, and Academy Award winners' previous spouses, it is distubring how little most believers know about their chief weapon of warfare. It's honestly not necessary to be able to recite the entire Bible from memory as some have done or even to recite whole books from it, for that matter. Nevertheless, it is important to know where specific principles can be found. It would be helpful to know the general thrust of each book in the Bible and to be able to find any book (Zephaniah, for instance) without having to fumble through the table of contents. Knowing a variety of specific verses and references for use in unexpected situations involving grief, fear, or personal evangelism could prove significantly worthwhile.

Christ used Scripture to resist temptation. Vietnam prisoners of war used it to keep their sanity while imprisoned alone in tiny cubicles for months or years. Other believers refer to memorized verses to make decisions and cope with uncertainty. That so many churches have stopped having children memorize Bible verses is scandalous. That they should reinstitute Bible memory work at once is imperative.

Likewise, a Christian should not only have a testimony but should be able to share it. It's difficult to be grateful to God or anybody else for gifts and kindnesses you've forgotten. It's equally hard to tell others about those forgotten gifts and kindnesses.

Finally, it goes without saying that spiritual warriors must be prayer warriors. The believer who doesn't pray often is admitting, at least to himself and God, that he

101

doesn't think it's important and that he obviously has lost his Christian perspective and fallen off the cutting edge. To use weapons most effectively one must know them intimately.

The effectiveness of one's weapons is also dependent upon the strategy with which the weapons are used. Here again, too many Christians and churches are woefully unprepared.

Mere common sense teaches that the offensive is the best position to take in any kind of conflict or competition. The old axiom insists, "A good offense is the best defense," and successful leaders from a variety of fields have always practiced that policy. It holds true in war, athletics, or politics.

For that reason football coaches train their players to rush out onto the field and initiate play in a burst of energy. They want their teams to explode quickly, to score early, and to score first. The team with the first score thereby gains valuable momentum while the scoreless team is subjugated to a defensive and inferior situation. In addition to everything else, the latter team is faced with the burden of "coming back."

The same is no less valid in matters of the military. By taking up the offensive an army or strike force is able to choose the field, time, and other circumstances of battle. Further, they are often able to catch the enemy off guard or at least less prepared. Consequently, effective generals from Alexander the Great to George Patton have sought the advantage of "first strike."

In the realm of the spiritual, valuable lessons in battle strategy may be drawn from the examples of Christ, Paul, and others of their contemporaries. They, too, realized the value of taking and keeping the offensive.

Christ controlled the battle lines of his ministry by boldly thrusting out in directions he deemed important. He never seemed dependent upon threatening situations or political circumstances. He chose where the skirmishes would occur. By the time the Pharisees assaulted him with dangerous questions, the very foundation of their existence had been shaken by his teachings. By the time the merchants in the Temple realized what had happened, they were sitting dizzily in the yard with their bird cages.

The carpenter from Nazareth never allowed others to place him on the defensive either. When critics infiltrated his audience and took the offensive with questions designed to trap him, he was totally disinclined to defend himself. Instead, he ingeniously turned the questions around, allowing the questioners to trap themselves. Even on the occasion of his trial before the Sanhedrin, an event wherein procedure called for a "defense," Christ declined. His profound silence left his accusers to flounder, flurry, and ultimately use their wicked designs in line with a divine purpose.

In his singular response to the Jewish Council, Christ's remark addressed his future glory rather than dignifying their charges with a defense of his past. When Pontius Pilate demanded that Christ defend himself and allow him, Pilate, to save him, the Nazarene replied, "You would have no power over me if it were not given to you from above" (John 19:11, NIV). In other words, "You only *think* you're in charge here!"

Paul, too, used his own courtroom defense as a means

of advancing the gospel. Not only could no one tell him when and where to preach and minister, but when they called him in to condemn him for disobedience, he used the defendant's bench as a pulpit as well. *Irrepressible* one might say!

Christ openly espoused the church as an assault force trained and willing to do offensive warfare in spiritual realms. A reexamination of his remark about the "gates of hell" not prevailing makes that clear. As a weapon, gates are defensive. Gates are used by militarists to delay the advance of enemy troops. Unlike spears or rifles, they are never used to attack an outpost or overrun guerillas. (The mental picture of gates being used offensively is quite hilarious.) Hence, Christ's original vision for the church was one of hell's strongholds being overrun and destroyed by His forces.

Somewhere between AD 30 and today things changed dramatically. Certainly the gospel is still being preached. Churches are still meeting regularly for worship. But it's different! There has been a distinct, if unintentional, change of strategy. Today's church, in her bid for respectability and status within the community, has lost her offensive edge. *We have allowed the world to put us on the defensive!*

Consider some of the most typical examples of the church at war in our generation. The teaching of evolution as scientific law rather than theory has now been accomplished in every public school in the land. Now, finally, the church has responded by defending her right to have "Creation Science" taught alongside evolution in public schools. Late and on the defensive, we find the momentum is against us. (And this still does not address the question of whether or not giving equal time to "our views" in public schools is the answer.)

We are now defending ourselves against more popular "thinkers" who have taken the spotlight at center stage while we have passively "fellowshipped" among ourselves. We have allowed our Christian consensus to erode. Not long ago in the United States it was the atheists and agnostics who were expected to defend themselves. Today they have achieved respectability, while Christians must defend their "narrow, ignorant, minority views" in the light of "secular enlightenment."

In the workplace, in the schoolroom, in the courtroom, and in the studios of Christian broadcasters, we go on blindly defending ourselves. We are not assaulting the gates of hell: we are too frantically engaged in fortifying our own. Worse yet, we are no longer looking so much to the needs of others as to the needs of ourselves. The bulk of our budgets is channeled into building maintenance, electricity for air conditioning, and other secondary matters.

Only very recently has the church begun to regain her perspective of the reality of spiritual warfare. In the intervening years, however, we have lost our offensive edge and have now begun to lose sight of our ministry too.

What can be done?

First we must dispel the worldly illusions that have come to surround us and take us in. Spiritual warfare is not simply an analogy for the timeless and passive contradiction between good and evil values. It is a real and ongoing conflict taking place on several levels in and

105

beyond our world. Something is definitely at stake, and souls are being condemned daily to hell.

Along those same lines, we must also discard the mind-set that suggests "It'll all come out in the wash." No doubt, God is going to win the war, but the territory is still being determined in "dogfights" around the world. The involvement of individuals does make a difference.

Secondly, we must rearm. We must return to our Bibles and refamiliarize ourselves with them. We should meditate upon some of those old clichés like "Love thy neighbor as thyself," and find their implications for our lives in this era. We should teach our children not only in Sunday School but at home. We should memorize Scripture together with them.

Churches must begin to teach not only the facts of the Bible but the *point* of it. Pastors must be clear in what God is expecting to accomplish through Scripture and through their sermonic efforts.

Some acquaintances of mine recently called on a young couple who had visited their church. The couple had previously been active in another church in another state. They mentioned how much priority they gave to study of Scripture and noted that their previous church had just completed a yearlong survey of the Bible. After such introductory conversation, how surprised my acquaintances were to discover that neither the man nor his wife were sure of their salvation. They thought they were saved by good deeds and church activities rather than through grace. *Here was a young couple who had been consistently taught the facts of the Bible but never the point of it.*

It is not merely the task of the church to teach people

about Scripture, prayer, evangelism, and caring. Our task is to *involve* them in those things. We must immerse our people in ministry!

Finally, we must cease being a "fellowship society" and resume our true identity as the church. We are not here to win members to a popular, fun-loving organization. We *are* here to lead disciples to a merciful and loving God. We are not here for the sake of "healthy church growth." We *are* here to influence, to teach, to heal. (Growth should be a by-product, but it was never intended as an end.)

The time has long come for Christians to take the battle beyond the courtrooms into barrooms, meeting rooms, dining rooms, recreation rooms, and beauty salons of our world. God never intended that the battle should be won through the courts. Indeed, the battle will only be won through his Spirit.

The church will begin to see victory when she changes the minds of judges, legislators, and voters; but the most thrilling results will come when she changes their hearts. Consequently, our primary thrust should be one of influence rather than litigation. Our task is one of loving, caring, and ministering so intensely that barriers are broken down and hearts are opened to the Holy Spirit of God.

As the salt of the earth we must seek to multiply the influence of Christ. As our influence grows, more and more people will become subject to the influence of the Holy Spirit. This is not to suggest political action groups. It is not to suggest the exercise of personal clout that one member or another might have with one legislator or another. What is called for is the kind of Christian influence the Bible talks about: *personal, life-style evangelism.*

Not only can we become effective spiritual soldiers, *we must!* No one could deny the dynamic ability of Jesus of Nazareth to evangelize men. "Now you are the body of Christ," Paul wrote to the Corinthians (2 Cor. 12:27), "and each one of you is a part of it."

We are the body of Christ who has the mind of Christ. We are promised by Christ that we can do even greater things than he accomplished as a man. There is therefore no excuse for a passive, sickly, inept, and defensive church. It is time once again to display the power of the resurrection.

But first we must liberate the prisoners of war. Thousands of Christians have been captured by worldly thought and secular perspectives. They think that all is well, that everyone is safe, and that the warfare is passive and merely symbolic. They believe that Good will ultimately triumph.

Though spiritually alive, they are rendered incapable of taking part in the battle. When the forces of Christ win they will share in the victory. But in the meantime, they sit behind barbed-wire fences of illusive, deceptive, and totally errant preconceptions. They are of no value to the cause. (In fact, like other hostages they are often used effectively for enemy propaganda.)

Once again the church of the Living Christ must take the offensive. There are priorities to be reorganized. There are illusions to be dashed. There are forces to be marshaled. When these things are prayerfully accomplished, the body of Christ can once again enjoy the momentum of *first strike!*

8. The Paradox of the Church

Paradox is nothing new to the church. We accept that during his earthly ministry Jesus Christ was fully man and yet fully God. At the same time we insist that man must consciously choose to become a Christian, we also assert that we were elect from the beginning of time. We understand that in spite of the fact that God is perfect and omniscient, he somehow created Satan. In matters of religion we have grown accustomed to the peaceful coexistence of seeming incongruities.

Perhaps it is for this reason that we have so easily assimilated yet another paradox, a *new* one that may be peculiar to present-day believers in this country. The new paradox?

Modern American Christians are the most active people on earth. They are also the most static.

When talking with friends or becoming acquainted with unfamiliar Christians, I too often find the general flow of information beginning to move in a very familiar direction. "We'd like to do . . . (one thing or another), but we're just too busy." "I never get to read anymore because I just don't have the time." Etc. Etc.

Whereas some people used to wear large crosses around

their necks to suggest their growing spirituality, they now use frantic scheduling for the same purposes. Christians are too busy to do things with their neighbors anymore. They're too busy to do volunteer work. They're even too busy (or so they insist) to watch television. The believer has become, or so many would have us believe, the twentieth century's authentic perpetual-motion machine. In the sixties, "go-go" applied to energetic girls who danced in short dresses. In the late seventies and eighties, however, the term has come to apply to fatigued Christians in their Sunday clothes!

What activity keeps these people so busy? Church, of course. We have been taught that there is something highly spiritual either to be derived or demonstrated through being at the church building every time the doors are opened, and these days those doors seldom close.

We attend Sunday morning Bible study, Sunday morning worship, Sunday afternoon Sunday School teachers' meeting, Sunday evening discussion groups, and Sunday night worship. And that's just Sunday. On Monday night there's deacons' meeting and women's groups. Tuesday night's agenda is visitation to call on Sunday's visitors. Wednesday involves more meetings, missions groups for kids and *prayer meeting,* commonly distinguished from Sunday's *worship* only in the smaller size of the crowd. (The three full minutes of prayer are generally a constant in both *worship* and *prayer meeting.*)

Thursday offers softball, basketball, or other recreation at the church building depending upon the season. Friday is slotted for parties for Sunday School classes and Bible studies for single adults. Saturday is filled with bus ministry meetings, other committee meetings, and youth activities which require adult supervision. There is something for every age group. *Every moment.*

Who could argue that today's concerned Christian is one of the earth's most active people? Consider at the same time, the *static* nature of the things in which that believer is so active.

Twice on Sunday he attends worship services wherein less than 10 percent of the participants conduct 90 percent of the goings-on. Simultaneously, 90 percent of the participants do little more than sit passively (or occasionally stand, but never longer than the length of a song and a prayer) through 75 percent of the activities. To many believers worship has more to do with the admiration of a talented choir or gifted speaker than with the expression of adoration and thanksgiving to a living, mighty, and awesomely eternal God. And no wonder.

One sits quietly through most of the act of worship. She sits quietly through Bible study. She sits quietly through prayer meeting. And he sits quietly through deacons' meeting, Sunday School teachers' meeting, Stewardship Committee meeting, Planning Committee meeting, Music Committee meeting, Building and Grounds Committee meeting, and Committee on Committees meeting.

Visitation too often translates into courtesy calls made for the purpose of inviting visitors and absentees to return to "our friendly church." *No evangelism or scriptural admonition, just friendly talk.* Just about as often, fellowship results only in more friendly small talk, this time among the faithful.

The question is not one of what *else* we can do to reach

111

the world. Instead someone must ask, "What are we doing now? *Is all of this rushing around truly justified?*" Are we honestly accomplishing eternal things through so many mundane meetings, or are we merely sacrificing our Christian influence in the community for the sake of making points with the pastor? Pastors should ask the question, "Am I demanding that my people live up to my expectations yet causing them to fall far short of God's?"

New Testament commitment calls for a life-style centered around the Christian faith. Failing to achieve that, we have too often substituted the local church at the center and the result has sometimes been pharisaical Christianity. We have implied that nothing spiritual can take place outside the church house. And in a *catch-22* situation, when we have called for ministry outside the building, we haven't left the people time to do it.

It's little wonder that in spite of all our money, education, and potential, the church is today losing ground. Our most dedicated members are hamstrung by meetings, paperwork, and the resulting fatigue. In all those hours at the church building, most of the time is spent in neither actual ministry nor in equipping members to do it. Too often there is only exhortation, glib flights of fantasy, and the misuse of statistical information. The tendency is to say that it's just as well because there's no time left for life-style ministry.

A friend in Texas once paid me a visit at the store where I worked as a seminary student. Our families were both involved in a nearby local church and both fell into that category of "dedicated, young, middle-class marrieds," the demographic set for which most every church is looking.

Pat had dropped by to share a frustrating dilemma our church was causing for him. He was a deacon, a Sunday School teacher, a member of the finance committee, a member of the choir, an expected participant in visitation, and one of those few often referred to from the pulpit as "a leader." He was committed to Christ, and he loved our local church.

Yet Pat was enormously frustrated because he had suddenly realized the disparity between the demands of our church and the demands of Christ. The church insisted that he be on hand at every service and every meeting. Even in meetings in which he was not a leader, he had a "ministry of attendance."

By contrast, Christ had called him to be the salt of the earth, to minister to his family and neighbors with whom he had unique influence. But he had no time for this. When neighbors called, Pat had to interrupt conversations in order to rush off to meetings at the church. When people invited him and his wife over for dinner, far too often they were already committed (weeks in advance) to a church social.

There was no time to tuck his daughter in bed with a Bible story because she was generally asleep when he arrived home. He was seldom with his wife. Either he was in a meeting and she was home, or he was in the choir and she was in the nursery.

Without knowing exactly how to voice it, Pat had stumbled onto a startling realization. He was hiding his light under a bushel: *his local church.* All his quality time available for ministry to family and friends, the people with whom he had the most influence, was being greedily gulped down by church bureaucracy. His hunger for service had been exploited and then paralyzed by *churchianity.*

It's not difficult to imagine how this situation began to develop. Perhaps it began with a few Christian leaders who didn't trust their people to minister on their own but didn't know how to motivate them. Maybe a few others helped to foster the excess through their own insecurity: if they couldn't see dramatic results at every meeting, they could, at least, measure things by the size of the crowd. Certainly, that old idiom must have come into play somewhere down the line: *"If one soul is saved because of this undertaking, all the effort will have been worthwhile."*

The possibility of saving one soul is no justification for the flagrant abuse of people's time, however. There are, after all, hundreds of ways in which a church could involve itself to save one soul. The prudent question should be, "How can we maximize our people's time to achieve the maximum amount of ministry for the maximum amount of people?" Involving six hundred Christians in an undertaking to win one soul may not be a true waste, but it is certainly not cost-effective stewardship. Any pastor should be able to win one soul on his own (in conjunction with the Holy Spirit) without multitudes wasting hours in meetings.

An interesting parallel to the present circumstance is found in 1 Samuel 15. The passage is the culmination of an ongoing narrative delineating the failures of Israel. The people were continuing to perform the rituals of their religion but had not allowed their faith to accomplish those things God had ordained it to accomplish.

In his response, God pointed out through Samuel, "To obey is better than sacrifice" (v. 22). Obedience to God is more important than rituals.

Like Israel we have sometimes been too eager to sacrifice for our faith. In the name of religious ritual we have given up money, time, family, friends, influence, and recreation. Yet, just as in the case of Israel, our rituals have become meaningless to God because we have ceased to be about what he is all about. We've no time left to be salt or light. We have no time to counsel or to make our marriages the kind of relationships God designed them to be. In spite of all our meetings, our churches are failing to measure up to God's standards for the church.

After all those years of hearing our leaders pray from pulpits, "Hide me behind the Cross," we have done just that: hidden! Behind crosses, behind stained glass, and behind towering walls of concrete and brick, we have hidden our faith and our life-styles and our concerns and our Lord. Small wonder our neighbors and families remain unimpressed. Either they are bemused by the pretense of our frantic flitting about, or they are vexed by the way we make such a fuss about "loving" them while taking absolutely no time to demonstrate it.

Preoccupation with the church may be one of Satan's most crippling illusions. Christians are more educated than ever before, and Bibles are more understandable, so it's a bit harder to lure God's people into theological heresy. We have more leisuretime than ever before, at least in the US, so it's more difficult for Christians to justify laxness in worship or service. So the kingdom of darkness has plotted a major switch in strategy. Instead of trying to keep Christians away from the church building, they now try to get them to go there often . . . *and spend all their time there!*

Brilliant! Under the sway of this new illusion, the faithful are allowed to feel deeply spiritual and highly committed. The unsaved, on the other hand, continue to walk in darkness but now with less hope than ever before. The Christian church, having overcome Gnosticism, pagan persecution, militant Moslems, and the Dark Ages, is now in danger of asphyxiation in her own cloisters.

If we are to reverse this deadly trend, the first thing that must change is our perspective. At the outset we must soundly reject this recent distortion that the local church is an end in itself. The local congregation is *not* an end in itself: *it is a means.*

The local church is a means of partaking in corporate worship with a tiny portion of the church, that church being too enormous and too widespread to afford congregation. The local church is a means of deriving the benefits of fellowship (encouragement, exhortation, shared concern) short of actually getting together with the whole church. The local church is a means of being prepared for ministry. Further, it is a means of mobilizing small pockets of believers toward that spiritual end of evangelizing the world.

That's not precisely the sort of truth the believers always hear about their congregations. To the contrary, Christians are frequently encouraged, at least implicitly, to focus on the local church. Saints who would never consider boasting about themselves feel not a tinge of shame in boasting about their local churches. Congregations position themselves in competition with neighboring churches. They target only their neighborhoods and pray only for their own sick.

We pray for beloved sister Alma's infected foot and implore God to intervene, yet we feel no responsibility to intercede on behalf of thousands of Christians being carted away to Russian labor camps in Siberia. We petition God for the new printing press we need to upgrade our weekly newsletter, oblivious to Third World believers who have no press, no newsletter, no church building, no Bibles, no shoes, no medicine, and little food. Most of us are very unlikely to pray even for local churches of our own denomination, much less for believers in other denominations, other lands.

One would think Paul had written, "For we are the *bodies of Christ,*" yet he didn't. He used the singular. There is one head, Christ. There is one body, the church. There are many diverse organs, the individual believers. In this Pauline analogy, the local congregation doesn't even have a place.

That's not to say that the local church isn't important or isn't biblical. It serves only to reassert that the local church *isn't an end.* Just as it would be immoral for a Christian to lavish all his time, money, talents, and energies on himself, it is likewise immoral for a local church to do so.

The local church is not a hiding place where Christians may cower in their pews in the face of the world's advance. It is not a spectators' booth where we may sit and offer

117

commentary while angels do spiritual warfare. The local church should be a launching pad where worship, discipleship, fellowship, and education create an atmosphere of readiness and confidence from which believers are hurled dynamically into lives of caring and ministry.

The local church is a means, rather than an end. It is not a ministry but a facilitator of ministry. It survives through supernatural power rather than manpower. It will enjoy the blessings of God once again only when members are looking outward instead of inward.

Having thus adopted a true perspective of the local congregation, we are now in a better position to consider the nature of our faith. Our faith is characterized in the Bible neither as a meeting nor as a series of meetings. Time and time again the writers of the New Testament depict the faith along a continuum. It is a walk. It is a race. It is continual advance.

Biblical faith does not revolve around meetings, for whatever their purposes may be. It does not revolve around circumstances or people or buildings. Instead, lives should revolve around faith.

Church homecomings and anniversaries can be painfully enlightening if not always delightful. When a few of the old-timers are asked to recount their fondest memories pertaining to that church, the incidents and accomplishments they recall will generally share at least one telling commonality: *they will all have occurred at the church building.*

By contrast, most of the things deemed memorable by Paul, Luke, John, and others took place on the highways and byways of life. True, there weren't a lot of local church buildings back then, but there were agreed-upon meeting places. And some significant things are naturally recorded as happening in those places, but love and concern were too powerful not to spill over into the streets. Had Paul ever resorted to the use of the phrase "a great time," he would no doubt have reserved it for something more stellar than sixty-five people showing up for a Thursday evening revival meeting to hear a humorous twenty-five minute message.

Perspective Adjustment #1: the local church is a means, not an end. *Perspective Adjustment #2:* life must revolve around our faith, but faith must not revolve around meetings or buildings. *Perspective Adjustment #3:* a true shortage of leadership in your local church is God's problem, not yours.

What? That last one was so shocking and peripherally heretical that a proof text is surely in order. "The harvest truly is plentiful, but the laborers are few," Christ taught his followers (Matt. 9:37). We can certainly relate to that problem, can't we? And what was Christ's prescription?

What he didn't do was unload additional burdens on the apostles. He didn't insist that the shortage of workers meant that these followers should "take up the slack." Instead, he placed the responsibility on God by instructing his men to ask God for additional help.

"Pray ye therefore the Lord of the harvest, that he will send forth labourers into his harvest" (Matt. 9:38, KJV).

In times of labor shortage, Christ's words instruct us to *look up.* But more often than not, church leaders and committees on committees say *bear* up. *Somebody's gotta change the light bulbs, teach the seventh grade Bible study,*

119

plan the Senior Adults' Christmas fellowship, and chair the Long-Range Planning Committee. No church can function without deacons, finance committees, outreach chairpeople, bus captains, nursery workers, hospitality hostesses, hymnal straighteners, greeters, choir members, and youth sponsors!

"We've only got sixteen regulars," comes the gripe. "Somebody's just gotta double up."

Double up.

Bear up.

Tighten up.

Hurry up.

Mess up!

Crack up!!

Done correctly, the work of a Sunday School teacher, for example, should demand all the free time a working Christian can afford. There's the thought and preparation which ought to go into every week's lesson: it *ought* to receive more thought and prayer than an hour or two. Then a Sunday School teacher should pray individually for her class members, visit them in their homes, and be conversant in matters that concern them. She should be there when they're ill and remember their birthdays and special occasions. She should call on new prospects for her class. Indeed, the Sunday School teacher fulfilling all of his or her responsibilities can honestly use every moment of available time.

Nonetheless, I think that, by and large, only faithful and dedicated Christians will accept teaching positions. They also happen to be the only people who will easily accept other positions, so every Sunday School teacher you'll ever meet (or let's be charitable and say eight out of every ten) will also hold several other positions in the church: choir member, Woman's Missionary Circle president, visitation clerk, Welcome Committee hostess.

By way of results, three possibilities are obvious. In Scenario A, she bears up under the continual pressure, but she is unable to do an excellent job in any area. Her lessons could be thrilling, but they are not. Her students fall away and are never visited or encouraged. She loses touch with their needs. Her prayer life suffers. Her husband grows to resent the church. She has no time to train helpers. So she muddles through, a committed and talented Christian, doing a mediocre job in several areas. *Mess up.*

Scenario B finds the pressures heightening. Problems at home require even additional time. The Sunday School class drops off so badly that the minister of education begins sending cute, but nagging, little cards and making friendly, but irritating, phone calls. The New Members' Banquet is a flop because of the teacher's lack of preparation. Finally, this woman with enormous potential blows up and stops attending the local church at all. *Crack up.*

More hopeful is Scenario C. Suppose this gifted Sunday School teacher had steadfastly refused to take on other responsibilities. When one leader or another came around with new jobs and "opportunities," she might have gently responded, "I can't possibly maintain excellence in my Sunday School class and assume additional responsibilities as well. But I will pray with you that God will provide a worker for that task."

Every believer should be willing to sacrifice for the kingdom of God. So glorious is our calling and so perilous

121

is the circumstance of each unsaved friend and neighbor that no committed believer should be content with a life of mere convenience. *But sacrifice should be for excellence, not mediocrity.* It is a far better thing to sacrifice for one crucial task and reap disciples than to sacrifice for a multitude of tasks and reap only the lackluster and mediocre.

Not a single pastor I know would suggest himself to be all-discerning or perfectly insightful. Most, in fact, are more than willing to admit their frailties and inadequacies. In spite of all this, dedicated Christians often seem to lose their grip in the presence of a beloved pastor with an "opportunity" to offer. Whether out of guilt, admiration, or simply inability to say no, Christians who care are all too likely to accept new positions even when they know there's no time left to handle them responsibly. Yes, it *does seem* that someone needs to do it and the pastor clearly needs a break.

In truth, the pastor's ultimate goals (and Christ's) might be far better served by a respectful refusal. Maybe the correct person hasn't been asked yet. Maybe the correct person hasn't been *saved* yet. Or maybe the program is no longer truly necessary and should be dropped.

Whatever the case may be, the answer will not be found in playing the martyr and striving for mediocrity. If God is omnipotent (as we believe he is) and deems the task important (if he doesn't, you shouldn't waste your time), he is far more capable of resolving the matter than you or I. "Pray ye therefore the Lord of the harvest," Christ taught, "that *he* will send forth labourers into his harvest."

Perspective Adjustment #4: God doesn't need crowds,

so don't wait for one. God didn't launch the Christian faith with the mass crucifixion of thousands. *One* was enough. (And when the Dark Ages saw the church grow fat and blind, one German priest was enough to launch the Reformation.) Evangelistic preachers, painting committees, and Meet-the-Budget banquet speakers need crowds, but God doesn't.

God can achieve the beginnings of excellence in your local church with only one person. Could that person be you?

Too often people who grow concerned about one thing or another decide to spearhead a crusade. Someone decides the people aren't friendly enough so he starts recruiting people to join him in demanding more friendliness. Or someone else decides that people aren't praying enough so he requests time after the service each Sunday night to harangue members about not praying. If one starts a crusade and gets everybody concerned, then things will change. Right? Not necessarily.

If nobody is praying in your church, the easiest way to affect change is by personally beginning to spend as much time in prayer as possible. Then at least one person will be praying and, seeing your results, others will follow. If nobody's friendly enough, don't wait for mass awareness and transformation. Become more friendly yourself. Explore new ways to show concern and acceptance, and at least there will be one truly friendly person in your church, which will be more than some churches have.

If everyone else is living at the church, there's probably nothing effective you can say to stimulate a correction in their thinking. *But you can affect change.*

Stop assuming new responsibilities that you don't have time or talent for. Take a spiritual survey. Discover your gifts and interests, seeking out the most effective way you can employ those gifts and interests in your local church. Estimate what will be involved in performing your task with excellence. Then schedule your time, providing adequate slots for devotion and meditation, family, church, neighbors, and your job. Having done that, pour your time into those elements of your life. Love your family with quantity and quality time. Go out of your way to encounter and grow more familiar with your neighbors. Do an exemplary job with the ministry you've accepted at your local church.

And having witnessed what God is doing in your life because you've dared to reject their churchianity, perhaps others will join you in life-style Christianity. But if not, at least you'll be making a difference. God hasn't called us to work only in crowds.

He has called us to be salt. And before salt can contribute anything of value it must be released from the shaker. Likewise, God's salty sons and daughters must first be shaken from their church buildings and back into the community if they are truly to be agents of the gospel. Deceived believers must realize the biblical role of the local church, a means rather than an end. The local church must be removed from the center of the believer's faith, and Jesus Christ must be returned to the throne of each life. Then we'll see salt, for when he *reigns* it *pours.*

9. Death Is Swallowed up

During World War II, one of Japan's most effective weapons against the advancing US fleet was her legion of kamikaze pilots. These young men, sometimes less than sixteen years old, were more than willing to crash their planes onto the decks and sides of US destroyers and aircraft carriers. Unbelievably, Japan seemed able to manufacture an unending supply of such young men!

Where did they come from? Why were they so willing to end their lives as human bombs?

History reveals that kamikaze pilots were taught that death for country would usher them into a land of boundless paradise. To die resisting the enemies of Japan, they were assured, was a heroic act which would be eternally honored by the gods.

Once a young man volunteered for such service, he was hurriedly trained as a pilot and then celebrated as a national hero for several weeks. Parades! Feasts! Any pleasure the nation could afford was at his disposal.

The selfless airmen were dubbed *kamikaze,* meaning *divine wind.* Popular thought compared them to cherry blossoms falling to their death in the late spring but making the earth fragrant.

The secret of the fanatical kamikaze was that all fear of death was programmed away. In a quick and intense wave of thought control, the young men were overwhelmed by nationalism, peer pressure, romance, legend, and seduction. They were taught that they had little to lose, everything to gain. They faced death unflinchingly at the whim of politician or militarist. The cause was just, and paradise awaited, they thought.

Today many of us might well feel some sadness for these teenagers so tragically manipulated by a desperate government. Japan was hopelessly losing her war, a particularly unjust war she had started. Such times called for desperate measures. Thousands died on the basis of patriotic fervor and the promise of paradise.

Ironically, many pastors of today are asking themselves, "How do you evoke even a hint of such devotion among today's church people?" And it's not a question of how to stimulate them to sacrifice their very lives. Instead, pastors and ministers everywhere are challenged by a more mundane dilemma: "How do you get them to give their *tithes?*" "How do you get them to share *some* of their leisure time?"

It should not be difficult. Indeed, Christians of days gone by have often been highly motivated. During the Roman persecutions, thousands of believers died when the mere utterance of yes might have saved them. "Yes, I worship Caesar above all others," was all that was generally required. They could have then gone home and worshiped Jesus Christ in secret.

But early Christians allowed their own words to seal their fates. They died for something as fleeting as truth.

126

Who could have blamed them for renouncing God under the threat of violent execution?

Undoubtedly, they surmised that God would.

First-century believers were taught, and rightfully so, that there was nothing to fear in death. Cruel and unjust death was the communion chalice from which untold legions of Christians drank willingly, not because they wanted to die but because they wanted to please God.

Perhaps one of the most profound and awesome prayers of the Bible is found in Acts 4. In the preceding narration, Peter and John had been brought before the Sanhedrin and were tried and beaten for preaching the gospel of Christ. When they were finally released, it was with accompanying threats of violence and death if they persisted in talking about Jesus of Nazareth.

Leaving the high council, the two men quickly returned to the company of their Christian friends. There they joined in yet another time of prayer.

First, notice the obvious things for which they didn't pray. They didn't pray for God to destroy the Sanhedrin. They didn't even pray for a pox on their accusers. They didn't pray for personal protection for themselves. And they didn't immediately begin guessing what new city God had in mind for their home. I can easily imagine my friends and me *spiritually petitioning* God for such things under similar circumstances.

Instead, consider the surprising thing for which they did pray: *boldness!* They asked God to give them boldness that in the face of these latest threats they might bravely preach the gospel.

"Lord," they didn't pray, "please help us raise enough

funds to send some missionaries out to risk their lives on the streets of this city! Lord, give us thousands and thousands of denarii that we may hire missionaries to boldly proclaim your Word in this treacherous town."

With a few administrative strategists around in those days, the first-century believers would seldom have needed to risk their lives. They could have instead launched a massive Sunday School expansion crusade inviting thousands upon thousands to come to Sunday School and worship, never once mentioning the name of Christ on the street.

They could have launched big visitation nights, paying calls on people who had already visited their little meetings. In most cases those would have already been believers; in which case, once again, the name of Jesus would not have borne so much as a mention.

Far too often there's a large obstacle which stands between most Christians and the practice of sharing their faith and effectively ministering. That obstacle is the fear of rejection. It perturbs our wizened little souls to think that other people might not like us if we do certain things. We might be considered strange, passé, or fanatical! And so commonplace is this concern that when we finally consider an act that strikes us as bold, we are generally considering an act which might cause us to confront possible rejection.

That is emphatically *not* what went on in the minds of Peter, John, and their fellow Christians. *Bold* in their minds did not denote risking unpopularity. It did not mean simply doing questionnaires in their neighborhoods. It did not involve driving one day a week for "Meals on

Wheels." It did not entail any of a number of cute, unique, and modestly beneficial activities through which one might loosely align himself with some of the teachings of a late teacher from Nazareth.

Bold meant facing death.

We are not challenged and inspired by early Christians because they were willing to be rejected. The world is full of neurotics who must daily deal with rejection. The Moonies face it. Jehovah's Witnesses risk it. American Communists, ecologists, tax collectors, telephone solicitors, and homosexuals are willing to face rejection daily and for a variety of philosophical, financial, and physical reasons.

The first-century Christians are remembered for their willingness to face death. They envisioned boldness as the readiness to publicly explain the good news of Christ to unsaved multitudes who could summon the executioners. Certainly they felt that worship could be a secluded and sometimes private thing but not their witness. A public witness was more important than life.

There is one fine point that seems crucial to one's understanding at this juncture. Implicit in the behavior of the church in Acts is the presupposition that even facing death was not enough. Instead, it was necessary that it be faced with abandon. A man balancing on a pole above a pit of deadly serpents is truly risking death. But early Christians might be more accurately characterized by a man striding recklessly through the pit to rescue a frightened damsel. The early Christians were not content merely to look Death in the eye: it was also important to spit in his eye!

There must have been dozens of surreptitious ways in

129

which the gospel might have been craftily proclaimed. Yet Peter, John, Paul, and thousands of their contemporaries chose the more public and direct approach. There was, of course, only one reason not to: death.

What did the early church understand about death? Indeed, what does the Bible say about death for those of us living out the faith today?

"He that believeth in me, though he were dead, yet shall he live," Christ explains in John 11:25-26. "And whosoever liveth and believeth in me shall never die."

There is something rather brash about making such a statement. Why *did* Christ say such a thing if he knew he could be contradicted? And if this was indeed disproved following the death of Christ and, ultimately, all of his apostles, why did writers and compilers of the New Testament leave it in?

Never die?

Apparently, both Christ and his chroniclers understood this to mean something beyond mere physical death—the expiration of mortal existence. Had he been nothing more than a charlatan, Christ would have certainly been intelligent enough to know a basic axiom held even today by a number of otherwise unenlightened modern politicians: *"Don't make specific promises that can be held against you later."*

Christ presented physical, mortal death as a transition, a portal through which one passes from life on one plane to life on another. That perception of death underlies his assurance in John 16:33, "In the world ye shall have tribulation: but be of good cheer; I have overcome the world."

Jesus of Nazareth was acutely aware of that other, larger, brighter sphere of life. Time and again he shoved his fist through the papier-mâché walls of temporal illusion in order to let something more dazzling, more real, shine through.

When he healed the sick and the lame—instantaneously —the promise of a grander reality sparkled through translucent despair. When he raised Lazarus from the dead, he opened wide a window to that other plane. And when he made such promises as, "In my father's house are many mansions" (John 14:2) or "To-day shalt thou be with me in paradise" (Luke 23:43), he unmistakably referred to reality as we don't know it.

Desperate though he was to alleviate some of the misery borne by others in this world's illusory existence, Christ was then (and is now) clearly powered by the priorities of that eternal sphere of living. There can be no other explanation for such unique teachings as those found in his Beatitudes. Yet it was more than the fact that his words were different. Christ's very bearing was different. Not merely his teachings but also the places he dared teach them totally set him apart from the hue and cry of Main Street religiosity.

He was so apparently brazen as to dine in the home of a reviled tax collector. He touched lepers! He dared allow a notorious woman to anoint his head and feet. His was such a boldly durable religion that it traveled anyplace with ease: all-purpose, one might say!

Christ's boldness far surpassed the act of unashamedly speaking about God, just as the boldness reflected in Acts denotes more than merely speaking unashamedly of Christ. Biblical boldness—holy boldness, if you will—

affects not only the proclamation but the connotation and the location as well.

The connotation called for is the obvious disregard for safety, ease, and mortal life. The bold witness permits his life to reflect heavenly priorities and eternal perspective rather than earthly considerations.

In the heavenly realm of thinking, eternal life is immeasurably more important than mortal life.

The location of our bold witness must be anyplace where the good news is not already being proclaimed. Certainly the church has been preaching the gospel in many parts of the United States, for example, for decades. But too often that preaching has been tragically localized in safe, middle-class districts and secure suburbs.

What of the ghettos and inner-city regions? What segment of the church is carrying the Word to red-light districts, drug havens, singles' bars, gay districts, and ethnic blocks? What Christians are daring to enter these forsaken places where lost multitudes congregate regularly? *Not many.*

"Heck! A person could get killed in a place like that!"

Certainly he could. But millions are already dying in just such places, and they're going to hell. Why is it that Christians give so much lip service to risking life and limb in foreign missions, as in the case of Jim Elliot's fatal mission to the Aucas, while discouraging any such risk taking at home?

Why is it more spiritual to die in an Amazon jungle than in a Detroit ghetto?

There's little reason to expect that Jesus, Paul, Peter, John, and their comrades would bypass the sleazy places

132

were their mortal ministries underway today. Indeed, every indication suggests those are exactly the places they would go. Boldness means proclaiming God's Word in just such places, without concern for possible death.

For too long, believers have avoided slums and ghettos because they were dangerous. Other places like bars have gone untouched lest the trespassing believer should "hurt his witness."

What a satanic lie! One can scarcely damage a non-existent witness; and that's what most safe, limited, middle-class "witnessing" has amounted to in the past. We want somehow to stand among healthy people and exhort them to health, but Christ exhorted us to carry the gospel to those in need of the physician. And there are far more sin-sick people in the places we avoid than in some of the exotic "mission fields" we frequent.

Arthur Blessitt characterizes the situation as "sending in the police to do our dirty work." The moral decay taking place across the tracks disturbs us. So we move our churches to the suburbs, establish mission churches in still other suburbs, and pay policemen to go in and bust heads in some sort of preventive fashion. But God's prescription for those people is not broken heads but broken, transformed hearts.

They need Christ. Of course that's credible for a Christian to say, and we've certainly heard it enough times to make it acceptable. Curiously, those pimps, druggies, punks, and gang members still don't believe it. If God can produce such transformation in their lives, why can't he muster the troops to deliver it personally?

"If God can overcome sin, guilt, aimlessness, drug addiction, and emotional scars," our unsaved ghetto multitudes must wonder, "why can't he deal with the cowardice among his own people?"

The reason is death. We're afraid of death. We can rationalize the matter by insisting that our families need us. Or we can spiritualize it by saying God didn't call us to that sort of ministry. Whatever our justifications, they won't hold water.

Should my daughter's life be threatened in some seedy part of town, my love and concern would tolerate no priority other than getting there, finding her, and doing something to rescue her. When it's strangers we're talking about, however, and it's only spiritual death they're facing, I suddenly don't know where to start. The enormity of the challenge overwhelms me. I'm afraid of death.

The first step for the Christian seeking to live in reality involves addressing death directly. That mysterious, ultimate inconvenience must be confronted as precisely what it is: an illusion. It is not necessarily painful. It is generally irreversible in human terms, but it is not final. Death is not a wall of separation but rather a doorway.

For the believer, death is instant access to the meaning of life: the essence of joy. In the kingdom of God, death is homecoming.

Paul's writings reveal that he had discovered and fully accepted the truth about this. "While we are at home in the body we are away from the Lord," he wrote in 2 Corinthians 5:6.

"You are no longer strangers and foreigners, but fellow citizens with the saints and members of the household of faith" (Eph. 2:19).

Paul understood the Christian to be a citizen of heaven. Even as he often claimed his Roman citizenship to gain quick access to new areas or to secure a fair trial, he was immensely more patriotic to the kingdom of God. There lay his true loyalty.

He wrote about it in absolute terms. His body was a worn tent, designed for and damaged by temporary residence while traveling. Life he saw as a race, an event with a beginning and end in the midst of a much grander and more significant existence. On different occasions he described himself as a runner and a soldier, both being short-term pursuits.

Death did not alarm Paul. He saw it as the ultimate opportunity in this life to sacrifice for God. He understood it as having been defeated, its sting removed. For him it meant the final approach to the awards bench where the trophies and laurels would be presented to the victors!

Living God's revelation to the fullest, Paul never deemed mortal life worthy of preservation, protection, or any sort of ultimate consideration. His life was nothing more than a resource to be spent in God's service.

Since it was God's resource, he focused on availability and left the matter of longevity to God. If the Lord had further plans for him in Ephesus, for example, he would not allow Paul's life to be snuffed out en route from Corinth.

Modern Christians wish to believe that such a world view is no longer viable or appropriate. We have convinced ourselves that life has become much too complex with overriding circumstances and underlying implications. There are long-term things like mortgages, wills, and family considerations at stake now. Right?

The problem is not the complications, but rather our love for those complications. We love life and the temporal things it offers. Nevertheless, our temporal pleasures are of no more eternal dimension than those rejected by Jesus, Peter, and Paul.

One of the reasons we fear death is because of the pleasant, temporal things it will snatch away. In contrast, Paul was keenly aware that eternity in heaven promises to overcompensate the believer for all those fleeting losses. He looked forward to oneness with God, endless joy, and a crown of righteousness which was laid up especially for him.

Much of what awaits any of us in heaven is never clearly described in Scripture. Yet in the matter of certain essentials, the Bible is quite clear.

Heaven is a place of unparalleled joy where one lives in the full, personal presence of God. It will never end. There will be certain rewards, not for our own pleasure but for the privilege of being laid at the feet of Christ in gratitude for his sacrifice. Heaven also offers consciousness and relationship. Family members who have made Christ the Lord of their lives will be reunited there forever.

Scripture also seems to make it clear that heaven is already a beehive of eternal activity. Even in our absence there's a celebration underway. Christians who are so obsessed with what they'll miss when they die might well be sobered to think of what they're missing right now by still being down here.

Death is the way most Christians will get to heaven, and

by that I mean earthly, physical, temporal death. That makes it not unlike a birth canal.

Sometime ago it dawned upon me that most unborn infants would probably dread their approaching birth if they knew what would happen. The average unborn is, after all, snug, warm, and in constant contact with a source of love and good feelings. His or her needs are met naturally as they arise. He or she is healthy and growing.

How would such a being feel about such an uncertain thing as "birth"? It involves nothing more than being squeezed slowly down a narrow tube to be hauled up in a blindingly lighted and antiseptically cold room for hurried snipping and slapping. Birth means being jerked away from mother and separated from her for hours at a time. One must cry to be fed; one must cry to be stroked. One must even wail incessantly to be relieved of those itchy, soggy, smelly diapers!

Ask an unborn how he or she feels about being born. He'll probably prefer the life he already knows, even though the rest of us would scarcely call that living. We'd call it mere existence, enduring the absence of an entire range of sensations and experiences!

Ask a Christian how he or she feels about dying. Hmmm. Sensations: undefined. Mode of transport: undefined. Eternal joys: undefined. A lot of Christians might deep in their hearts prefer their comfortable, well-defined, mortal life-styles. God doesn't call that living.

Evangelism Explosion, the training ministry with which I'm affiliated, centers on two questions. The first is simply, "Have you come to the place in your spiritual life where you know for certain that if you should die tonight you'd go to heaven?"

The answer to that penetrating question ought to separate the men from the boys and the women from the girls. A sincere answer of yes ought to be the most satisfying, exhilarating experience within the mortal range of experience. Suddenly the greatest threat this life can make against one is permanently snatched away. The ultimate weapon of fear and intimidation is once and forever unloaded. The person who answers in the affirmative is in a no-lose situation.

Either I continue to live mortally, or I begin to live eternally.

David penned a profound metaphor in his twenty-third Psalm when he spoke of walking through "the valley of the shadow of death." There is no threat in that valley—no mechanism for harm—only the illusion of such. David saw death as a shadow—a dark, uncertain place through which one might temporarily pass with assurance. He emphasized that there was nothing to fear.

Believers have nothing to fear in this earthly, physical phenomenon we know as death. Rather than an end, it is a new beginning. It offers access to ultimate fulfillment, revelation, fellowship, and joy. It provides transition to a state of oneness with God. And it ushers the believer into a position of enjoying these things on a permanent basis. Death is the believer's eternal birth canal.

Christian life-styles and ministries should reflect the fact that we have no illusions about death.

10. The Overcomers

What would the world be like if caterpillars refused to emerge from their cocoons? One could certainly understand the reticence of an imaginary caterpillar named Ollie. A few weeks ago he was just another fuzzy little worm. He had stripes, tiny antennae, lots of stubby legs, and an insatiable appetite for leaves. On impulse one day, Ollie began chewing even more than usual and an odd thing happened: *he found himself weaving a cocoon.*

Before long Ollie was all wrapped up in his work—*literally.* Bundled securely in a soft, warm, little package tailored to his torso he idly laid around for a few days. Then came sleep—gentle, seductive slumber. Days elapsed. Weeks passed.

Now Ollie finds himself awakened by the shouting and buzzing of familiar voices. He recognizes the sounds of his parents and friends urging him to come out and play. They're shouting that he must come out and look at himself. Why are they teasing him, Ollie wonders. Why are they saying he must come and try his wings?

Ollie knows he's just a homely, little, squirmy squirt with two dozen left feet. He's seen his reflection in the brook before. Why should he come out of his comfy little sock just to see reflections of that same old face he's seen so many times before?

He's certainly seen himself enough times to know he doesn't have wings—doesn't even have a place for wings! Caterpillars don't fly!

"Go away!" Ollie shouts to his friends outside. "Go away and leave me alone! I'm just an ordinary caterpillar who crawls slowly and looks kind'a dumb. I'm never coming out of this cocoon!"

Ollie has undergone a radical change and he doesn't understand it yet. He's no longer the same creepy crawler who snuggled into that cocoon a few weeks ago. Through a process that totally mystifies both him and all of us, a once chubby and clumsy caterpillar is now a slender butterfly with glorious, graceful wings.

Ollie's colors have changed. His appetite has changed. The way everyone will perceive him has changed, and even the laws of gravity won't apply in the same way anymore. He can now enjoy the miracle of flight.

Ollie will never fly though. He'll never soar through the heavens from blossom to blossom or dazzle watching children with his beauty. He'll never feel the invigorating lift of the breeze rushing against his broad wings or experience the unique reality of being a butterfly because he will never come out of his cocoon.

What if he burst forth from his fuzzy shell and leaped into the air only to be dashed cruelly against the earth—still an ordinary caterpillar? He might be crushed underfoot. Or worse, he might have to finish his life as a caterpillar, never able to return to his safe little cocoon again.

Some Christians have the symptoms of Ollie's problem.

140

Everyone tells them that their conversions, their rebirths, have changed them. Supposedly, their natures have changed, their interests are altered, and their desires are different. The Bible insists that a whole new series of principles and laws applies uniquely to them. *Can it be true?*

Can it be true that the Holy Spirit is now dwelling in young John who prayed with an evangelist recently? Does he really have the mind of Christ and the power of the resurrection, or is that just religious double-talk?

John hasn't nearly memorized his Bible yet, but he's read enough to know that it makes some claims just about as preposterous as caterpillars sprouting wings. Casting mountains into the sea, it says! "I can do *all things* through Christ who strengthens me" (Phil. 4:13). For real?

John has been informed that he's inherited eternal life and that his whole life has changed. Many of the rules that apply to other men don't apply to him anymore. He could be in store for miracles.

But like Ollie Caterpillar, John will never experience the joys and rewards of his new life because he's afraid to come out of his old cocoon. What if he should race into the Christian life, embrace all of its radical principles and then *fall flat on his face?* Where would he turn if he made a leap of faith trusting God to catch him, *and God didn't?*

One might characterize our fictional friend John, as well as the many other churchgoers like him, as *living beneath his privilege.* The sublime is available to him, but he settles for the mediocre. He's like a man who wins a brand-new Rolls Royce but continues to drive only his '62 Volkswagen lest he get a dent in his new Rolls!

It makes for a baffling situation. On the one hand, an individual professes to trust Christ enough to rest the entirety of one's eternity in his hands. Christ seems to be reliable and trustworthy in matters of eternity, something that lasts forever—never ending. On the other hand, more people seem to have less confidence in that same Jesus to handle temporal, day-to-day cares and concerns. He can be trusted with the unending totality of eternity but not with the mundane and often insignificant events of everyday life? *Absurd* is too mild a word for that proposition.

Through prayer, meditation, and consultation with older and wiser Christians, someone like John may discover that he's truly a believer but needs the encouragement and edification of fellowship and corporate worship in order to grow more rooted in his faith. It may be that no one ever told him exactly *how to proceed* after the prayer with Reverend Sweet that night.

John may discover, however, that he has trouble trusting Christ from day to day because he has never really trusted him for eternity. Perhaps in his unfamiliarity with spiritual things, John heard "Ye are saved by grace through faith," but then understood "Ye are saved through prayer." Reverend Sweet kept insisting that he needed only to pray.

"This prayer can change your life, John. Won't you pray with me now and ask Christ into your life?"

So John gave in and expressed a prayer. And then he expressed some fleeting hope. But he never expressed *faith,* and a prayer without faith is nothing more than mumbo jumbo, voodoo ritual, incantations, or bad poetry. Christians become just that through grace and faith. A prayer leads to Eternal Life when it expresses faith; without faith it leads almost nowhere.

In faith, Christians are called to more than a mere existence. We are called to an adventure! We are invited to join in a hearty, robust, thrilling, and sometimes dangerous odyssey. Through faith we must be ready for anything, not because fate is so fickle but because God is so limitless. His power and wisdom are so matchless that he cannot be predicted or second-guessed.

Faith is important to the believer on this journey not only because of what it accomplishes at the destination, but also because of what it accomplishes along the way. We don't know what's around the next bend, how fast the currents are, or how deep the water is. We're not certain if there are 'gators in the water, rocks just below the surface, or snakes along the shore.

God *knows.* He has given us principles and guidelines which enable us to avoid safely, circumvent, or overcome all the deadly pitfalls along the way. And faith, *absolute confidence in his authority,* enables us to follow those directions even when they seem mysterious or inscrutable.

Confident in him, we can rejoice even in great personal tribulation. We can defuse confrontations and convert them to witnessing opportunities. We can set aside our own rights, trusting God to compensate us generously either here or later. We can return to him the tithe of our income, even when finances are unusually tight. Through faith we are able to accept the whole Word of God.

That sounds like a very "churchy" thing to do, accepting the *whole* Word of God. It must be tougher than it seems, though, because there are far more congregations who talk about it than who actually do it.

Some congregations demonstrate, shall we say, a heightened sensitivity to the Holy Spirit. Not only do they believe in him, but they actually seem to worship him alone. They plead for him, praise him, and pray in him to the virtual exclusion of Jesus Christ. They can easily accept even the "hard teachings" about the Spirit. What they fail to accept is the true biblical perspective that the Spirit never glorifies himself but always glorifies Christ.

At the other extreme are the congregations who seem unusually sensitized to our sinful world. So intently aware are they of sin in the world that they are continually decrying it from their pulpits. Every sermon, every lesson, nearly every comment is a derogatory tirade against this sin or that individual, this demonic lie or that gross heresy. So determined are they to remain unspotted by the world that they can scarcely get along with anybody outside their congregations and many within them. They daily affirm the judgment of God but regularly preempt the love he has called his children to demonstrate even toward sinners.

Between those two poles stand most of the rest of us. Some of us can accept everything in the Bible . . . except the teaching on divorce. Some accept everything . . . but the miracles . . . or the subordination of wives . . . or the negative teachings on homosexuality. Still others write off God's judgment and hell, the exhortations to live simply, the admonitions to witness, or the prohibitions against gluttony. No strange and unenticing frog in a biology lab has ever been dissected, segmented, and desecrated so thoroughly as has been the sacred Book, the Bible, at the hands of believers.

Yet one of the most striking values to come out of this three year consideration of biblical perspective has been my increased awareness of *the unity of God's Word.* Everything interrelates. Rejecting one principle or another is not unlike pulling a snagged thread in double-knit slacks. It may seem unsightly and unrelated but pull that thread, and you'll immediately find a gap running through the whole fabric.

So interrelated are the Bible's principles that at first, it seemed that this book's direction might be very circular and overlapping. For instance, one can scarcely discuss the biblical view of death without spilling over into the principle of suffering. Personal suffering, of course, begs for additional treatment of God's view of rights and responsibilities which ought to be a separate chapter. Spiritual warfare certainly deserves a chapter to itself, if not an entire book, yet it continually overlaps with the topic of God's view of religion and the church.

Hence, it would seem virtually impossible to live a balanced and effective Christian life while either overtly or implicitly rejecting even one or two important facets of Scripture. Pull out one and you've weakened the biblical support for all the rest. Human beings have already learned that they cannot play favorites with other elements of God's creation. Kill too many coyotes and the rabbits destroy the region. Cut down all the trees for farmland and you lose the precious soil as well. So intricate and infinitely considered is the divine blueprint for the cosmos that no element can be segmented and isolated. *In the kingdom of God, things do fit squarely together.*

During my memorable days as a young seminarian, I devoted one semester to a chaplaincy internship at the New Orleans Parish Prison. A rather quiet and unassuming (read "naive") young fellow, I would never have signed up had I even suspected that chaplain interns would go *inside* the cells. Nevertheless, I signed up first, learned the truth later, was too proud to chicken out, and, consequently, was assigned to cellblock D, a block with four tiers (floors) of inmates.

Day number one found me timorously making my entry into D-1. The men were quiet, fairly polite and respectful, and they requested prayers, money, phone calls, money, and the usual chaplainlike services. And money. (We could pray and make phone calls for them but were *never* to give or lend money.) Day number two spent on D-2 was equally tranquilizing. Things went well; the guard responded to my knock and let me out within a reasonable period of time, and my confidence began to soar.

The next day was scheduled for my introduction to the men of D–3, a crowded dormitory tier badly cluttered with rusty bunk bed frames, dirty mattresses, hanging clothes, and photos and scrawlings of nude women. I had confidently made my way to the rear of the large room and was totally obscured from the guard's view (guards never watched interns anyhow) when I met Leroy and Spider.

Rather quickly I discovered that Spider was in for rape and robbery and Leroy was in for armed robbery and murder. How could I help them? they laughed bitterly. Unless I could give them some money or let them out, a little jerk such as I could help them not at all I was quickly informed. Tension rising, they began to insist that I should give them some money. I laughed nervously and offered to pray. (At that point, I needed it more than they.) Then after a few more minutes, Leroy stalked angrily away leaving me to continue my seemingly fruitless discussion with his friend Spider.

Then he returned. Leaning so closely to me that I could feel his breath against my face, Leroy called my attention to a long, pointed object held menacingly under his shirt. I had heard enough stories from the chaplains to believe his assertion that this was indeed a knife and that he was willing to cut me in two if I refused to give him the money I had with me. Despite the fact that we were speaking rather quietly at the rear of a dimly lighted tier wherein most sight lines were obscured, virtually every inmate on the tier had assumed a vantage point from which to watch this drama. All eyes were on me, the skinny kid from Alabama with the knife pointed at his ribs.

In honesty, I must confess that my first thoughts were not heroic visions of glorious martyrdom. In fact, my very first thought was, "What if he only wounds me and shoves me under the bed! How will I ever get out of here?"

Eventually, I began to recall the reasons for which I assumed God had brought me here. One of them was to glorify him. So, taking a deep breath, I informed Leroy (no doubt rather squeakily) that I had precious little money and was forbidden to give him even that. I think I said something about if the choice was one of my money or my life, he'd have to take my life. (Aggggghhhhh!!)

Not surprisingly, I didn't look at my watch, so I'm not

certain how long this standoff lasted, though it seemed interminable. Finally Leroy smiled knowingly and walked away. I finished my conversation with Spider and left the cell.

Then I determined to return to D–3 on the following day. The experience had been terrifying, but I realized that my impending ministry to those men depended on my continuing response to what had happened. Day number four found me waiting nervously at D–3's heavy door with the tiny barred window while the guard fumbled with his keys and released the lock.

Once inside, I found two dozen inmates immediately swarming to my side. Fortunately, I suppressed an impulse to shout for help and found myself being ushered toward the dimly-lighted rear section of the dormitory. There Leroy motioned for me to have a seat on a bunk. With inmates sitting in a circle around me on the floor and on bunks, Leroy smiled and said, "Talk to us, Preacher Man."

From that point, my finest and most rewarding opportunities for ministry came with the men of D–3. Leroy and Spider became my strongest supporters and most willing assistants.

As it happened on that fourth day, I was scheduled to preach in the chapel service on the following Sunday. Weekly services scheduled at 8:00 AM, had become an event attended only by a handful of inmates. But on this Sunday guards were amazed by the unusually large turnout. Surprised chaplains suddenly realized that D–3 had turned out *to the man* for worship!

Leroy later told me that the knife had only been a long

piece of cardboard. I'm sure he was telling the truth, for I came to realize that only a foolish con would risk having his knife confiscated by brandishing it before a strange new chaplain intern. Yet on that frightening first day in the shadows of D-3, everything told me that the knife under Leroy's shirt was all too real.

On that day, Satan tried to hinder my work with all kinds of clever deceptions which seemed to preclude the overcoming power of God. This was the cell with the most hardened criminals in the entire prison: Why should they be kidding around? The guard couldn't even see me to rescue me had he cared to look. What could God possibly salvage from this grim scene? *Only one of the most productive and intriguing ministries with which he's ever blessed me!*

"Be of good cheer," Christ urged his apostles during a time in his ministry when it seemed that the jig might be up. The Pharisees and Herodians were openly plotting together against him, and his own men were growing more and more baffled and disturbed by his teachings. Yet even at this unsettling moment in their ministry together, Christ dared to suggest that they lighten up.

"Be of good cheer," he charged them, *"I have overcome the world"* (John 16:33, author's italics).

Even before the trauma of the crucifixion or the miracle of the resurrection, Christ laid claim to having overcome the world. This initial victory came through his confidence in his father as well as his refusal to live by the world's standards. Worldly principles held no sway with him: not simply because he was the perfect Son of God, but because *they were only lies.* They remain so even today.

That opportunity so clearly enjoyed by Christ, the chance to overcome the world now belongs to this generation of believers. Ours is the capability to climb higher, to live more intensely, to experience the blazing reality of eternal love. We can conquer our world. Indeed, "We are *more* than conquerors," Paul wrote, "through Him who loved us" (Rom. 8:37).

The adventure begins with the transfer of one's trust from himself to Jesus Christ. It continues with a firm commitment to abide by the principles of God regardless of circumstances or misgivings, to sink or swim according to God's Word. Not illogically, it may involve being misunderstood by people along the way.

My favorite analogy for this situation involves two prisoners living in the total darkness of an underground cell— a black hole, if you will. After seemingly endless months or years, the first man suddenly shouts, "Light! I can see a light overhead! I see a light!"

The second man sees nothing. He attempts to calm his fellow inmate, his eyes searching the darkness above him all the while but futilely. Still the first man goes on in his excited shouting about the newfound light, much to his cellmate's irritation.

Short of actually resolving the dispute, at least two possibilities are evident. It may be that Man #1 has gone to pieces under the strain of his cruel imprisonment. As his fellow inmate insists, perhaps he sees only the delusions of his weakened mind.

Or maybe Man #2 is blind.

God tells us that the second choice is often the case. Unbelievers insist that there is no light, that there is no

150

substance to Christianity other than illusion and superstition. They insist that we are dissatisfied with our imperfect and evolutionary world and have, as the result of that dissatisfaction, created an imaginary God to balance the scales for us.

Yet the Bible explains why they should logically feel that way. Certainly they cannot see the light. They are blind.

For unenlightened eyes, life can offer an overwhelming abundance of painful and discouraging sights. "Welcome to the real world," the cynics quip when some idealistic innocent is suddenly crushed amid his high expectations. Only in the domain of carnal man does reality end.

The real world, the kingdom of God, is a place of mercy, meaning, joy, and victory. It is a sunny place where the impossible isn't. Through the grace of God, mortal men and women may enter this timeless and orderly kingdom even while walking among the illusions of the natural world. And in this mysterious transition from nature to supernature, we find that the real world is a wonderful place in which to live.

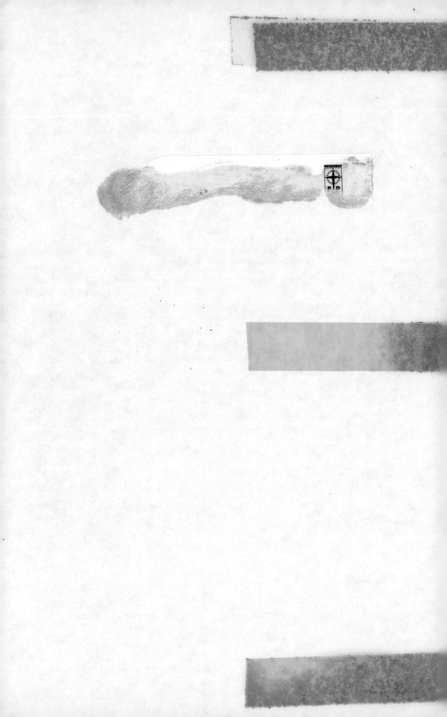